D1008750

AUTHENTICITY

AUTHENTICITY

The HEAD, HEART,
and SOUL of SELLING

RON WILLINGHAM

PRENTICE HALL PRESS

PRENTICE HALL PRESS
Published by the Penguin Group
Penguin Group (USA) LLC
375 Hudson Street, New York, New York 10014

USA • Canada • UK • Ireland • Australia • New Zealand • India • South Africa • China

penguin.com

A Penguin Random House Company

AUTHENTICITY

ISBN: 978-0-7352-0534-5

An application to register this book for cataloging has been submitted to the Library of Congress.

First edition: May 2014

PRINTED IN THE UNITED STATES OF AMERICA

10 9 8 7 6 5 4 3 2 1

Text design by Ellen Cipriano

I dedicate this book to Dr. Overton Faubus, who was supposed to be teaching me accounting, but from whom I learned much more about life thanks to his example.

If I were to list ten names of people whom I have valued and admired the most in my lifetime, his would certainly be among them. His humility, wisdom, sincerity, disciplined example, and genuine interest in people touched thousands of students, many of whom became highly successful business leaders.

What a spiritual giant he was, and is, and will always be.

DIMENSIONS OF
THE HUMAN PSYCHE IMPACTING
YOUR SALES PRODUCTIVITY

Head (hed) *n*

The conscious mechanism that holds opinions, knowledge, reason, memory, logic, and imagination. Exercises judgment and willingness; chooses direction and use of time, resources, opportunities; and makes good and bad decisions.

Heart (hart) *n*

Represents the emotional part that exhibits moods, levels of happiness, sadness, depression, elation, devotion, sympathy, love, joy, and peace. Withholds or gives love. Measures the attraction or rejection of other people. Supports or trumps the decisions, actions, or opinions that are made in the *Head*. Often overrules logic and discipline.

Soul (sol) *n*

An entity that is regarded as belonging to the immortal or spiritual part of the person and, though having no physical or material reality, is credited with having a major unconscious influence on the functions of thinking and acting and on determining the deeper causes of all behavior.

CONTENTS

INTRODUCTION

How This Book Can Help You Increase
Your Sales and Quality of Life

*The psyche, as a reflection of the world and man,
is a thing of such infinite complexity that it can be observed
and studied from a great many sides.*

—DR. CARL JUNG

Who can understand the human psyche? *Why* does it function like it does?

To make my point, let me tell you about a couple of friends. The first one was a very nice and, from all outward appearances, highly successful man. He'd just had his best business year ever. He seemed to have it all—a beautiful family, lots of friends, recognition from his company, a new two-story home in an upscale part of a large city, more money than he'd ever earned before. His highest goals and dreams had seemingly been realized. Walt Disney would've wanted to film his life.

Then why did he go to the men's room of an adjoining office building, put a gun to his head, and pull the trigger, leaving everyone stunned and totally devoid of explanations?

I'll tell you more about him later.

Contrast his story with a salesperson who reported to him. He was in his late twenties when I first met him, selling financial services, married with two children, earning a modest income. He enjoyed helping people gain financial security. It gave him a deep sense of meaning, knowing that he had helped save people from possible financial problems. As he tasted the joy of helping people, he later decided to go into the ministry. He did, and is very happy and fulfilled today.

What goes on inside people's psyche? Why the vast contrast?

The real question is: *"Why do we choose to think and do what we choose to think and do?"* We know a little about how the mind works, but in the face of our measureless human complexities there's still much more to learn. One thing I've learned—the more we learn, the more we learn there is to learn.

Especially as it relates to selling.

Let's explore that.

Let's move past "how to sell" and think about the heretofore unknown knowledge, emotional, and spiritual factors that make up the "why" we sell.

Complex Drivers of Human Action

There seem to be forces at work within us—beyond our knowledge—that cause us to create the quality of life we unconsciously believe we *deserve* to enjoy. Our actions, feelings, behavior, and abilities are generally controlled by these inner guidance systems. Our deep sense of worthiness seems to dole out to us qualities of life that we unconsciously believe we deserve to enjoy.

These become inner belief boundaries—mental, emotional, and

spiritual paradigms. They're programming from our life experiences that form self-beliefs—whether true or not true—to be deeply imprinted well behind our veil of consciousness. We live them out through values we were taught or not taught. Spiritual resources we have or don't have. Emotional influences that seem to come out of nowhere.

These and other nonlinear, illogical elements tend to motivate 85 percent of our actions, feelings, and behavior.

And . . . our resulting sales.

This should be a bombshell discovery for anyone in sales, or sales management. After observing tens of thousands of salespeople in my courses, I'm convinced it is true.

This book digs deeper into the fundamental forces that drive your sales, beginning with your *purpose*—why you do what you do, think like you think, believe what you believe, and perform like you perform.

Your Purpose Priorities

You'll be refreshed and excited about the following selling purpose priorities:

1. To create the most value for the most people, and then
2. Expect and receive compensation that's consistent with the value you create.

Successful selling is doing things *for* people, not *to* them. *Helping* instead of *persuading*. *Serving* instead of *being served*. This new definition, paradoxically, increases your sense of purpose and meaning, client loyalty, and sales.

Selling Redefined

Moving from old traditional persuasion-focused selling to a more professional client-focused strategy, here's my definition of selling success:

1. Success in selling is seeing as many people as you can to see who wants or needs your help. If they want or need your help, you help them. If they neither want nor need your help, you haven't failed; you've succeeded in finding out whom you can help.

2. Failure is finding people who want or need your help, but you won't help them. It's also failing to contact people who might need your help because you're afraid you can't relate to them, or they might think you're just trying to earn money off them.

When you internalize this definition, you'll feel empowered, and be freed emotionally to increase your contact activities. I'll help you take this definition from knowledge to automatic application as we go through this book. As you apply these two practices, you'll first feel an intellectual transformation, then an emotional one, and finally, as your deepest spiritual dimension embraces it, it will send higher levels of energy and confidence throughout your being.

How This Book Can Help You Enjoy Increased Success

More than an informational book, I've written this to be a weekly guide for your personal and sales growth, not just to read to gain knowledge, but to apply success principles that yield results for you. When you apply and practice the actions I'll share with you, you'll enjoy the following benefits:

- Attract clients because of your sincere desire to help them.
- Uncover new strengths and abilities that have been buried within you.
- Connect with all personality types and levels of people.
- Listen customers into buying.
- Have people say, "I want to do business with you because of who you are."
- Handle disappointments and setbacks.
- Release inner emotional toxins that clog up your energy and drive.
- View selling in a whole new professional role, adding to your stature.
- Redefine your role as helping people, rather than selling to them.
- Believe you should be compensated consistently with the value you create.

Now, before we go further, let me emphasize an important overall point that will then guide our thinking throughout this book. We'll look at the whole of what it takes to successfully sell and break it down into its different facets for you to understand and practice.

Whole-Person Selling

Observing many salespeople, I believe that selling can be divided into these percentages.

- 15 percent *Head*—knowledge of products, systems, and industry application.
- 85 percent *Heart* and *Soul*—feelings, emotions, values, inner belief boundaries, and alignment with spiritual truths.

I'll lead you into integrating the Three Levels of Consciousness—*Head*, *Heart*, and *Soul*—into your selling. As this occurs you'll enjoy these benefits:

- Learn a new paradigm for successful selling.
- Integrate all your mental, emotional, and spiritual resources.
- Acquire new levels of personal power.
- Infuse you with a fresh new enthusiasm that helps you overcome obstacles.
- Chase away fears of failure or rejection.
- Motivate you with a new, vibrant inner sense of meaning.
- Expand your view of your actual possibilities.

Probably for the first time in your sales training you'll learn about and work on these deeper issues that drive most of your sales performance. You'll discover and access more profound dimensions within you than you've previously known about.

Let's examine some deeper causes that have major influences on your success.

The Human Psyche

Any student of human behavior has discovered that there's a lot going on inside us that we don't comprehend. We know, learn, speak, and make decisions. At the same time we can feel and be happy, sad, depressed, or elated. We dream and have sudden insights, hunches, and creative thoughts that seem to come "out of nowhere."

Sometimes we do what we know is right, and other times we do what we know is wrong. We even seem to have different personalities depending on our changing social setting.

Who can figure all this out?

The well-known psychologist Dr. Carl Jung writes and explains a lot about human action. One of his beliefs was that each of us has residing in our unconscious dimensions an intelligence he called the *spirit of truth*. He believed we each have an inner, spiritual intelligence that discerns truth from nontruth. This spirit of truth encoding came with our "original equipment" as creative human beings. When we make decisions or choose actions that are congruent with this inner spirit of truth, we're *integrated*, or *balanced*, and we have greater emotional and physical strength. As this happens, increased personal power results. Not because of what we *know*, but because of the confluence of the three parts of us—*Head*, *Heart*, and *Soul*.

Only in recent years have we learned how to develop a much deeper understanding of our latent inner powers and design workable processes that integrate and implement them to drive increased sales performance. Most training and coaching are still aimed at directly changing the *effects*, rather than first changing the *causes* that produce them—effects such as: Manage your time better. Close more sales. See more prospects. Work harder. And so on. But these usually don't change until the attitudes, beliefs, and behaviors that drive them change.

The following model is a matrix, or a framework that helps us understand the deeper actions and reactions taking place within the human psyche that influence our performance. You'll learn more about the interworkings of this model in most of the coming chapters.

The Three Levels of Consciousness

To simplify the vastly complex human psyche, let's remember that each of us is made up of three parts: *Head, Heart,* and *Soul.* Your *Head* represents the conscious intellectual dimension. Your *Heart* is the emotional part of you. Your *Soul* is the unconscious, creative, spiritual essence and intelligence within you.

The following model is the central message of this book. It brings to you a new understanding of the forces within you and how they each influence your performance. Increasing the efficiency of this system becomes a central theme we'll weave throughout this book.

Please take a moment and study the following model:

THE THREE LEVELS OF CONSCIOUSNESS

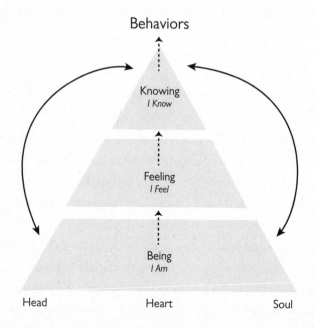

Behaviors

Knowing
I Know

Feeling
I Feel

Being
I Am

Head   Heart   Soul

This model shows the different parts and interaction taking place in the whole of the human psyche. Here's a quick definition of each dimension, and then in later chapters, we'll continually build your understanding of this model's application to different issues that drive real-world selling.

Your *I Know*

Your *I Know*, your *Head*, is your conscious, logical, decisive, intellectual level that learns information, makes decisions, and solves problems. With it you have product, industry, and technological knowledge. But have you ever noticed that you don't always do what you *know* to do, or even do what's in your best interests when strong emotions block you?

Most formal education and training employ passive information-oriented teaching processes, much of which gets forgotten within a few days. Only a small part of it is converted to habits or automatic behaviors.

Your *I Feel*

Your *I Feel*, your *Heart*, is the emotional dimension within you. You can feel up one day and down the next. Try as hard as you might, you can't always control your emotions with willpower or knowledge.

Your *I Feel* will overrule your *I Know* around 85 percent of the time, especially in selling and self-management activities. Ever set a weight goal, only to be faced with a hot fudge sundae sign on the restaurant table? Which won: you, or the sign? Ever dread contacting a disgruntled customer, so you put it off, and then put it off, and then . . . ?

But as powerful as your emotions are, there's still a deeper, more profound level within you that controls most of your emotions, which then trigger your choices and behaviors. This part gets little notice, and its vast powers generally lie undiscovered and unused.

Your *I Am*

Your *I Am*, your *Soul*, is the creative, unconscious, spiritual part of you. It houses your spirit of truth, values, sense of worthiness, belief boundaries, life force, spiritual and emotional thermostat, and creative mechanism. It's the Miracle Intelligence that heals wounds and connects you with the Infinite. This is the same invisible Intelligence that keeps acorns producing oak trees, corn kernels producing cornstalks, the earth on predictable rotation, and the cosmos responding as directed by its Manufacturer.

This is the infusion of Intelligence within you as you were created in the image of God. It intuitively knows what truth is, and what's right and what's wrong. When our decisions and actions are consistent with truth, we are physically and emotionally strong and empowered.

Strong, positive emotions, personal power, and energy are established when these Three Levels of Consciousness are integrated or in harmony with each other.

My main objective of this book is to assist you in bringing these three levels into harmony or congruence. As this happens, you'll automatically perform on much higher levels, you'll enjoy expanded qualities of life, and your productivity will expand.

Your Inner Sense of Worthiness

As you'll learn on several levels throughout this book, the chief driver of your decisions and actions is your inner sense of worthiness—the extent to which you unconsciously believe you *deserve* to enjoy life's rewards.

Each of us has our own self-definition chiseled on the walls of our inner being. Based on our response to our life experiences, we each make decisions about who we are, how good we are, and what level of success and rewards we deserve to enjoy. Then, whatever this assumed, unconscious self-definition is, we live it out without questioning its authenticity.

Whether they're right or wrong, these accepted beliefs become "truth" to us. And because we unconsciously believe them to be truth, we automatically perform consistently with them. This "truth" becomes a self-fulfilling prophecy, creating internal congruence or conflicts. Unfortunately most people go through life not knowing this, and having no help or reason to understand and change their "truth."

Most great thinkers have come to believe that this sense of worthiness is built by the value we create for others, rather than by what they can do for us. A paradox—a seeming contradiction—as many spiritual truths are.

Interaction Between Levels Creates Emotions and Behaviors

You'll notice that in the model, the arrows going from your *I Know* to your *I Am* create a connection that then produce your *I Feel* emotions. When your conscious choices are congruent with the beliefs, values, and spirit of truth in your *I Am*, positive emotions result. Your emotions, either positive or negative, are often so strong as to support or overrule your decisions, choices, actions, or behaviors.

Contact avoidance, call reluctance, and fear of rejection are great real-world examples of this interaction torpedoing our sales efforts. These shatter sales success more than almost any other factors.

Whenever the choices, decisions, or actions from your *I Know* are *consistent* with your values, belief boundaries, and the encoded spirit of truth within your *I Am*, positive feelings and energy are unleashed in your *I Feel*.

When there is a congruence between the three levels, emotional constraints are removed, and energy expands and overrules your fear of taking action, replacing old, natural fears with free-flowing confidence and expanded activity levels; unshackling you to do activities that bring higher sales production. Transforming contact anxiety and its emotionally killer cousins into result-producing activities directed toward helping people who need you.

On the negative side, when the choices of your *I Know conflict* with the values, belief boundaries, or spiritual truth encrypted in your *I Am*, negative emotions are triggered. Fear. Anxiety. Worry. Insufficient activity levels. These can neuter your knowledge, wreck your willpower, and demoralize your discipline around 85 percent of the time.

Dr. Leon Festinger, of Stanford University, coined the term *cognitive dissonance* years ago. It means having mental or emotional conflicts. He helped us understand these inner conflicts and how they can block us from reaching our true sales and earnings potential. This helps us understand the extent to which our values and unconscious self-beliefs influence our decisions and actions.

You'll learn ways to move through these mental and emotional conflicts as we go through the book.

Integration of the Three Levels of Consciousness

When there's harmony, integration, or congruence between your intellectual, emotional, and spiritual levels, you'll enjoy many benefits, such as the following:

- An expanded state of *flow*, being *in the zone*, or having a *second wind* physically and emotionally.
- Increased confidence, sense of meaning, and purpose.
- Positive beliefs, thoughts, outlook on life, and attitudes that crowd out and replace negative ones.
- *Attractor fields* that you exude, naturally drawing people to you like magnets to iron.

In short, as this congruence occurs, your whole level of consciousness will be gradually transformed. You'll become a more effective person. Increased mental, emotional, and spiritual energy develops and is at your command. Your brain waves change, as does your physiology or cellular makeup, according to many research scientists.

The CLIENT-Focused Sales System

Study after study has shown a bewildering fact of human nature: We're hardwired to enjoy greater meaning, joy, and happiness when we view our life role as serving others. Yes, I'm quite aware that this directly conflicts with our self-focused, ego-driven natures. I have plenty of my own problems with that.

There are the two opposite decision poles within us—self-absorbed and others-focused. These constantly fight for control of our lives. One *promises* rewards, recognition, and acclaim. The other *delivers* meaning, peace of mind, and spiritual discernment.

After writing a client-focused purpose statement in Chapter 1, you'll learn a six-step system to carry out your purpose of creating the most value for the most clients. The system gives you a complete process for completing sales and self-coaching steps.

Here are the six steps:

1. CONNECT: Gaining comfort, trust, and rapport with clients.
2. LISTEN: Diagnosing clients' wants, needs, or desired solutions.
3. ILLUSTRATE: Explaining how you can help clients enjoy their desired benefits.
4. EVALUATE: Making sure your solutions are right for clients.
5. NEGOTIATE: Working out problems that keep clients from buying.
6. TRANSACT: Exchanging your solutions for clients' payment.

You'll learn about these in Chapter 3 and then spend a week working on each one in Chapters 4–9. I'll encourage you to apply them in your daily selling activities, eventually developing them into automatic habits.

A positive transformation happens to people who practice our CLIENT-Focused Sales System. It's self-rewarding in three ways when you sincerely practice it:

1. Your intent to create value for others releases endorphins and neurotransmitters into your brain, influencing your emotional and physical well-being. More about these in a moment.
2. Your clients trust you because of your sincere desire to help them, and they reciprocate their feelings and trust back to you.
3. A trust bond is established between you and your customers that benefits both of you by creating a win-win relationship.

Oh yes, you also sell more.

These inner power surges add a whole new dynamic that very few salespeople, or their clients, have the opportunity to experience.

According to the research of noted experts like Dr. David Hawkins, when your values, choices, and actions are in an emotional and spiritual congruence, *endorphins* and *neurotransmitters* are released into your brain. Endorphins can reduce pain and stress and promote calmness, providing a consistent flow of positive energy and "feel-good" emotions. Neurotransmitters such as dopamine and serotonin contribute to pleasurable emotions much as certain drugs do. They can have significant effects on emotions, moods, anxiety, and sleep regulation. They leapfrog you over emotional blocks and barriers, nurture your *I Am*, and enliven your senses, transforming work into an anticipatory pleasure.

These effects certainly validate client-focused selling.

You Should Be Highly Compensated

Most of us who sell are motivated by money.

Practicing what you'll learn in this book will definitely help you earn more, if you're compensated consistently with your sales production. No, not just reading it, but applying the processes in it. I'll share examples of how real people who practiced the CLIENT-Focused Sales System enjoyed substantial sales and income increases.

Let's be honest. We like to provide well for our families, enjoy some of life's pleasures, give to our favorite charities, and save for a rainy day. Nothing wrong with that. The question is, how do we go about earning enough to do this? What's the cause, and what's the effect?

I believe we should be compensated consistently with the value we create for others. If you believe that you should create a lot of value for your customers, then you should expect to earn a lot for doing it. The issue isn't about whether we create high value for clients or earn high incomes. They aren't mutually exclusive. They can go together—when our priorities are right.

It's Mainly About Quality of Life

This book isn't just about increasing your sales. It's also about helping you expand your *quality of life*—answering the cry of your *Soul* for *purpose*, *significance*, and greater *life meaning*.

I'll be your "printed coach," taking you by the hand and walking with you step by step through the chapters of this book. If you take action and follow my directions, I promise that you'll see changes in your selling success and related rewards, whether they be money, advancement, customer loyalty, or other tangible and intangible benefits.

But I must warn you: You can't just *read* this book and expect these great benefits to happen to you. You must *Read. Absorb. Practice.* This takes commitment, application, and time. No shortcuts.

I've carefully repeated important points from time to time throughout the following chapters. This isn't due to senility; rather it's because most of the principles are learned on many different levels, depending on where you are in your progress. The mind that read Chapter 1 will not be the same mind that reads Chapter 6 or any others.

So how about it? Are you ready to take this transformative step into increased sales and quality of life? Are the rewards of increasing your career and life effectiveness more compelling than the costs of time and effort you'll need to give? Will you not allow common doubts or old limiting pictures of your possibilities to stop you?

"Yes," you say. Then jump on board, and let's lift off.

BLESSINGS,
RON WILLINGHAM

PART I

LAYING A STRONG FOUNDATION

A man is the façade of a temple wherein all wisdom and all good abide. What we commonly call man, the eating, drinking, planting, counting man, does not, as we know him, represent himself, but misrepresents himself. Him we do not respect, but the soul, whose organ he is, would he let it appear through his action, would make our knees bend.

—RALPH WALDO EMERSON

PURPOSE

*The intent to serve others strongly activates the right brain
chemistry and physiology. This alters perception and releases
anabolic neurotransmitters and endorphins into the brain.*

—DAVID HAWKINS, MD, PHD

Your intention changes your realities.

A graduate of one of my courses in a large hospital in Florida felt stuck in an unexciting job of making and serving Jell-O. Every day, she dozed through the same old, same old. Not only was her job boring and routine, but her life seemed to have no real purpose. After all, how much creativity does it take to make, portion, and display Jell-O?

This is the way it was until she learned to switch her thinking from *what she did* and focus on how much other people *enjoyed what she did*. As she began thinking about the pleasure she brought to people, rather than the boring, routine daily work activities involved, her whole attitude and job satisfaction completely shifted.

At her course graduation, she began her talk in front of her classmates by saying, "I have the best job in the world!" Her sincere beaming smile and animated gestures tended to prove her assertion and showcase the total transformation she'd experienced.

She went on: "I get to make little kids and older people happy. They love *my* Jell-O. Little kids don't just eat it, they like to roll it around in their mouths, and slurp it and squiggle it. They like all *my* flavors. And older people love *my* Jell-O. For some of them, that's all they can eat." She had much more to say about the joys of her job but ended her talk by emphasizing, "I have the best job in the world . . . I get to make people happy."

What a difference. A life-changing one for her. A total transformation.

What made this difference? Simple. She now had a different reason *why* she worked. A new, exciting, meaningful *purpose*.

How did her *purpose* change her?

Why did it change her?

Contrast our Joys of Jell-O person with a friend who came into my office one day, looking like his favorite team had just lost the Super Bowl. Frowning, not looking at me, he mumbled a greeting, sat on the edge of a guest chair, wringing his hands, and without any preliminary chitchat, said, "I borrowed some money at the bank and bought a distributorship for these automobile safety devices."

He paused, took a deep breath of air, and went on. "The note is due today, and I haven't sold enough to pay it off."

I quickly got the drift of where the conversation was going and waited for him to continue.

Painfully and pleadingly, he finally looked up at me and asked, "Would you buy one of these from me, so I can pay on the note?"

He was a good person, and I sincerely felt sorry for him. I had bought one from another friend, so I had a reason for rejecting his offer without rejecting him. My cowardly side felt sorry for him and wanted to loan him some money, but my better judgment slapped my hand, and I didn't offer that.

I'm sure he left my office with less hope than he had when he came in.

What was his *purpose* that day?

How did his *purpose* influence his sense of worthiness?

Your Purpose Is *Why* You Sell

Each of us has a *purpose* for what we do—whether we're aware of it or not. Studies show that more than 80 percent of working people find no energizing, exciting, fulfilling purpose in what they do. That percentage is probably even higher for salespeople. My observation of salespeople all over the world is that the more their purpose is to get people to buy from them, whether it's the right solution or not, the less job satisfaction they enjoy.

This self-focused or survival purpose offers no hope for a greater tomorrow. Or for a greater today, either.

I always wonder if their customer satisfaction follows the trend line of their job satisfaction. I'll bet it does. If it does, this isn't great news for companies that aren't customer-focused.

A few years ago, 28,000 Chevrolet salespeople in 900 dealerships went through my course. The more manipulative their selling tactics had been, the more I saw high turnover, low sales performance, and low customer satisfaction numbers. Although we didn't do statistical studies, I was convinced that some of their contrived, manipulative sales strategies also contributed to higher substance abuse and divorce rates. Personal, emotional, and spiritual corrosion seemed to follow inseparable career erosion.

Many of the salespeople had been taught to do goofy things—like meeting people coming into the dealerships with the question, "What can I *sell* you today?" As if this phrasing would trap the person into buying. All sorts of manipulative strategies were employed—all pitting salespeople against customers.

Our people trained sales managers to train their salespeople to welcome customers and spend time gaining rapport with them and understanding their vehicle needs and usage. Only then would they recommend specific vehicles that would best serve their needs. In an initial test with twelve dealers of all sizes, their closing ratios went from one in five to one in four. Their negotiated gross profits increased 31 percent. Customer satisfaction numbers skyrocketed. We even saw deeper personal growth in many of the salespeople, such as quitting smoking, losing weight, reconciling marriages, or earning promotions.

Our courses finished with a graduation dinner. Participants brought spouses, friends, and guests. One of the dealers in a large midwestern city had included all his salespeople, managers, service writers, and body shop estimators in the course. The graduation was conducted in an upscale country club, with an elegant dinner. Each of the participants came to the front of the room and shared what they'd gained from the course, how they'd applied it in their jobs and life, and what their future goals were.

After one serviceperson made his talk and was on his way back to his table, and the rousing applause had died down, his wife stood up and, in a very loud voice that could be heard for miles, announced to the group, *"And he don't come home and beat me no more!"*

Can you imagine the hush that fell over the room? Yes, it really happened. One of our staff was there and heard it. There was probably an interesting conversation at their home that evening.

Let's hope he didn't renege on his recently acquired discipline.

Your Selling *Purpose* Drives *How* You Sell

Why do you sell? What's your *purpose*? Your *intent*, *motive*, or *reason*?

Why you sell (your selling purpose) will determine *how* you'll sell (your strategy). Your selling strategy then will strongly influence your actual sales. Is your intent to persuade people to buy whatever you want to sell them? Or is it to understand their current and desired situations to see if they want your help, and, if they do, to create the most value for them? Are you self-focused or client-focused? Each intent produces its own strategies. Each strategy produces its own outcomes.

Not only will you sell more, but when your purpose is congruent with strong, positive service values and ethical imperatives, you'll enjoy high confidence and energy. Your self-beliefs and success expectations will be elevated. A wholeness will develop between your *Head*, *Heart*, and *Soul*, creating internal power. An aura of sincerity will radiate from the inner you, attracting people to you, causing them to want to do business with you, and strengthening trust relationships.

Let's begin by thinking about these four typical purposes, or focuses, we see in salespeople—each being driven by a different purpose or intent.

1. Client Focus
2. Transaction Focus
3. Product Focus
4. Survival Focus

Here are some results, or implications of the four different sales focuses:

1. *Client Focus:* You have the client's interests in mind. Your goals are to understand what wants or needs they may have, and to determine whether your solution it the best one for them. Your whole focus is on them, creating the most value for them, and thankfully receiving the compensation generated for the value you created. Ironically, long term, this is the highest-income focus.

2. *Transaction Focus:* Your main focus is closing as many sales as you can and reaching goals you've set. Your focus is mostly on yourself—how much you can sell and earn to reach your goals. This focus is reinforced by contests, incentives, and other rewards for closing sales. Nothing wrong with this, unless you are mostly concerned about what you'll earn from the sale and have little interest in asking yourself, "Is this the best solution for the customer?"

3. *Product Focus:* You see yourself selling specific products or services, rather than creating value for customers. Your conversations are more around your product features rather than on the benefits your clients will enjoy. While a lot of commodities and well-known products can be sold this way, relationships often aren't valued in this focus.

4. *Survival Focus:* Many of us get on financial, personal, relationship, or job security survival levels from time to time. We may feel pressed to sell something to avoid some bad outcome. It's difficult to have true empathy with customers when we're consumed with selling enough to pay our bills, getting terminated from our jobs, or keeping the other shoe from dropping. A survival focus tends to block out our ability to focus on clients.

Your Intent Is Unconsciously Communicated to Customers

Something within your customers' unconscious radar screens intuitively picks up on your true intent. You'll communicate it. You can't hide it. It's communicated through your instinctive levels, and while customers may not logically, consciously define it, they unconsciously sense it through feelings and intuitions. (We'll get into this more in Chapter 4 in the first step of our CLIENT-Focused Sales System.)

People intuitively pick up on whether we want to help them or sell them. They consciously or unconsciously observe our body language, eye contact, and other physical signs that reveal our intent. We communicate our purpose on a much deeper subliminal, *Soul* level. Our intent to serve invites acceptance, openness, and trust. Pressure to get people to buy creates counterforce, push-back, or unconscious resistance.

Each of these four sales focuses carries out a specific purpose that then supports or restricts our energy, confidence, and actual production.

It all begins by how we define what we do, or what our view of selling is. Ask different salespeople what they do, and you'll get answers like the following:

- A *client-focused* person says, "I help people enjoy," and then mentions the end-result benefits they help clients receive and enjoy.
- A *transaction-focused* person broadcasts, "My goal is to earn as much as I can, and I'm here to get you to buy something so I can earn more."

- A *product-focused* person signifies, "I'm here to tell you about my product or service features and benefits, with hopes that you'll buy it."
- A *survival-focused* person silently screams, "I hope I can sell someone something so I can make my house payment."

Most of us have been in survival modes before. It's difficult to move past it, as it's so self-reinforcing. We tend to spend most of our time defensively: Focusing on what we don't want to happen. Trying to put out problem fires. Plugging up or dodging challenges that scream for attention. Sucking positive energies out of us. Preoccupied with ourselves, rather than on how we can help customers.

Whichever focus you're on, the solution is to begin doing client-focused activities. Sooner or later this will move you toward a success level.

Scientific Studies

Dr. William A. Tiller is a world-renowned professor emeritus of Stanford University who has produced more than 250 academic papers. He came to the attention of nonacademics a few years ago when he was a part of the popular video *What the Bleep Do We Know!?*

Dr. Tiller's interests led him into scientific research about how the power of *intention* alters matter. One of his experiments was changing the pH of water by placing it in the vicinity of an electrical device that had been imprinted with that intent. His conclusion was that human consciousness can change matter.

For our practical, nonscientific application, let's translate this into my belief that our intention, or purpose, tends to change our realities, as well as other people's responses and internal perceptions of us. For instance, when our *intent* is to help people who need our help, we change their receptivity of us compared to when our *intent* is to persuade them to buy from us. Our intent can literally create either positive or negative emotional charges in us that are communicated to our customers, which generally change their responses to us.

One course participant, Keri Kalka, a genuine, caring person, shared with me how she'd strengthened her intent to help more people who needed her advice. In her work as a financial advisor, this carried over into all of her activities. Her values supported this belief, our course gave her the process for helping people, and she felt she should help as many as possible.

Unlike many other financial representatives, who are reluctant to contact their friends or family, she felt that these were people she should be most interested in helping. She made two large sales to a close family member and a friend. Her growth showed up in all parts of her life. She concluded a letter to me by saying, "I am so happy that I can hardly contain it. I've been waiting a long time to finally reach my stride and to be the person that God had in his mind's eye all along."

Changing her intent changed her outcomes.

Can just changing your intent or purpose actually alter your success in selling?

Mull this question over as you read and study this chapter. See if you don't develop your own answer to it.

Okay, let's begin at the beginning—writing out a client-focused purpose statement.

Writing Out a Client-Focused Purpose Statement

A client-focused purpose statement finishes this sentence: "I help clients enjoy . . ." with the benefits you and your products give clients, and *how* you do it. For example, your response might be:

> "I help organizations enjoy greater efficiency by providing them with state-of-the-art software for their accounts receivable."

> "I help people enjoy greater financial security by saving money and insuring against future risks."

> "I help people enjoy greater economy and safety by helping them select the best vehicle that fits their individual driving situations."

This statement becomes your marching orders. The *what* you do. The *why* you do it. The *who* you are. The *how* you operate. It becomes the passageway through which all your sales efforts are directed.

Take a moment and write out your purpose statement. Refer back to my sample statements.

C'mon, don't get lazy on me. Please stop your reading and write out your purpose statement.

Your Purpose Statement Becomes Your Elevator Speech

Your elevator speech is your answer to anyone, including yourself, who asks you, "What do you do?"

When you get up in the morning and the person in the mirror asks you, "Well, good morning, who are you and what do you do?" How do you answer him or her?

Your answer can easily predict your day. If your answer to the person in the mirror is similar to this, you're going to have a great day:

"Thank you for asking. My name is Mary Brown, and I help people plan for retirement so they have peace of mind and know their future is secure!"

The person in the mirror will probably respond:

"Well, thank you, Mary, I can tell that you're going to have a great day. You're going to feel good about who you are and what you do."

But if your answer is similar to the following one, you're probably not going to have such a spectacular day.

"Why are you asking me this question? You know I sell computers."

The person in the mirror will probably say:

"I'm sorry for bothering you. Maybe you should go back to bed."

What's the difference?

One is telling yourself and others the benefits you help your customers enjoy. The other is telling them what you sell. Both purposes will influence how you feel and what image you communicate. One strengthens. The other weakens. Which one do you want to experience? Who makes your choices for you?

The more value you give people, above the price they pay you, the more confidence, self-respect, and inner sense of meaning you'll enjoy. Clients will respect you more. Have greater trust and loyalty to you. Want their friends to buy from you. See you in a different light than they see your competitors.

Let's take it to the next step.

What Benefits Do Your Products or Services Give Your Clients?

This is an incredibly important question to ask. To answer it, though, you need to be looking through your customers' eyes, rather than through your own. First, realize that you have totally different motives for selling what you're selling than your clients have for buying what they're buying.

You're enthralled with the great features of your products or services, as they're often your differentiating factors when pitted against your competitors. You view these features as your unique factors, so it's natural that they are what you want to talk about. But these features are important to your customers only to the extent that they will help them enjoy the benefits *they* want.

This is where disconnects often occur, and what keeps you and your clients on different wavelengths. You talk about what interests you—your product or service features. You forget to talk about what interests them—how these features will help them get the results they want.

More on this later. You'll continue discovering the actual benefits that your clients want to enjoy, as you go through the chapters ahead.

Let me share with you why focusing on clients' end-result benefits is important.

The Law of Psychological Reciprocity

This law makes the point: People are instinctively compelled to return to us the same attitudes and behaviors that we exhibit toward them.

This means that:

- When we listen to people, they are impelled to listen to us.
- When we sincerely want to create extra value for people, they get the message and instinctively want to return value to us.
- When we genuinely want to understand people's needs, wants, or problems, they tend to trust us more and want to buy from us.
- When we seek to see the worth in people, they are instinctively compelled to see the value and worth in us.

This law really kicks in when you implement the CLIENT-Focused Sales System that you'll learn in Chapter 3. This dynamic law guarantees success for you when your true selling purpose is to create the most value for the most people.

The Great Paradox: What Gives Us a Stronger Sense of Meaning

Let's think about some wise words from experts in human behavior. You read the following statement from Dr. David Hawkins in the opening of this chapter, but it's so important that I want to repeat it, and ask you to stop and meditate on it for a few moments. It contains a whole new level of understanding of interpersonal communication.

David Hawkins, MD, PhD, may have discovered more about human behavior than anyone else in the last century. Author of many books, he wrote this:

> The intent to serve others strongly activates the right brain chemistry and physiology. This alters perception and releases anabolic neurotransmitters and endorphins into the brain.

When our *intent*, the *why* we sell, is to *serve* others, some amazing transformations take place within our *Head*, *Heart*, and *Soul*. Our thinking changes. Our bodies are transformed.

But that's not all.

Jorge Mill and Jordan Grafman, neuroscientists at the National Institutes of Health in Bethesda, Maryland, scanned the brains of volunteers and concluded that when these people placed the interests of others before their own, their generosity activated a primitive part of their brains that usually lights up in response to food or sex.

Now, that's a pretty remarkable brain change.

Paul Bloom along with his wife, Karen Wynn, did a study of babies at Yale University. Bloom wrote an article for the *New York Times*, stating:

> A growing body of evidence, though, suggests that humans do have a rudimentary moral sense from the very start of life. With the help of well-designed experiments, you can see glimmers of moral thought, moral judgment and moral feeling even in the first year of life.

He concluded by writing:

Babies possess certain moral foundations—the capacity and willingness to judge the actions of others, some sense of justice, gut responses to altruism and nastiness.

Viktor Frankl, MD, wrote in his classic *Man's Search for Meaning* that the strongest motivator of people is the need for meaning. To count for something. To make a difference. To express our unique gifts. Our sense of meaning is enhanced when we know that we give more than we take—serendipitously creating a surplus in our emotional and spiritual bank accounts.

He found that his patients enjoyed significant improvement in emotional and mental health when he got them reaching out to help make other people happy, and got their focus off themselves.

Is there a message here for salespeople? Absolutely! We have a name for it—client-focused selling. We also have a process for doing it, which you'll soon learn.

Allow me to emphasize: Anything that impacts human behavior influences our selling. So we must always look deeper than knowledge or conscious thought. This involves understanding deeper workings of our emotional *Hearts*, and spiritual *Souls*, which begins with our purpose, or intent.

Hardwiring Permeates Our Whole Psyche

Numerous studies give evidence that we are actually born *hardwired* to enjoy greater life meaning as we serve and create value for others. This hardwiring has been installed in our spiritual *I Am*, or

Soul dimension, and then permeates our whole psyche. Our choices to honor its encoding by making decisions and choosing behaviors congruent with it bring positive results. Paradoxically, it's in the ethical choice of serving that we enjoy the greatest sense of meaning.

New energy levels, confidence, and emotional go-power are released from the spiritual holding pens within us when this is our intent. These potent success drivers are dampened when we try to sell people by persuading them to buy from us, solely for our own benefit. Our souls are cheapened to the extent that we pressure people to buy from us.

John Cato confessed to me that before he began practicing our CLIENT-Focused Sales System, his main purpose was to beat the other salespeople and win his company's contests. He saw clients as notches in his belt, helping him reach his sales goals, so he could earn more money and win contests. When he began to focus on client needs, gaining rapport and listening to them with the intent of helping people who needed his help, he began to feel much better about himself. With this change in purpose, his whole countenance changed, caused by a vastly improved self-worth. He made two sales that he wouldn't have made without practicing the CLIENT-Focused Sales System. His income more than doubled the previous year's earnings, and he did well then.

Now, we all need to earn money to pay our bills and eat. Frankly, there have been many times that my strongest motivation was to sell something because of my own survival needs. I can tell you that it didn't contribute to my confidence or sense of significance at the time. Knowing what I now know, I'm sure many of my clients got the message that I was focused more on myself than on them.

The main antidote for these times is to give as much energy to practicing client-focused selling as we can, believing that this is the best way out of a survival stage.

Redefining Success in Selling?

In the Introduction, I briefly defined selling as follows. We breezed through it then; let's delve deeper now.

1. Success in selling is seeing as many people as you can to see who needs your help. Should they want or need your help, you help them. If they neither want nor need your help, you haven't failed; you've succeeded in finding out whom you can help.

2. Failure is finding people who want or need your help, but you won't help them. It's also failing to contact people who might need your help because you're afraid you can't relate to them, or they might think you're just trying to earn money off them.

I challenge you to write these definitions out on an index card or your electronic device. Memorize them. Think about what they mean. Evaluate your application of them each day. Gear your selling activities to be consistent with these definitions.

You'll see a big change in your activities, relationships, and results as you begin practicing these definitions. The *who* you are will change on the inside and be evident to your customers on the outside.

Over the years, I've done muscle testing on hundreds of people by having them hold an arm out parallel to the floor, clench their fist, and resist my downward pull. When they say, "Selling is helping people," their arm strength is extremely strong. When they say, "Selling is getting people to buy things from me," they test very weak.

Even repeating the word *sell* causes muscles to get weaker.

Verbalizing the word *help*, as in helping create value for people, immediately causes arm muscles to get stronger.

This conflicts with conventional wisdom and the way most salespeople are taught to sell . . . but it's true.

This simple arm strength exercise is involuntarily controlled by the *hardwiring* in your *Soul*. You can't consciously control it with all the willpower in the world. Your inner *spirit of truth* controls it.

Could it be that something deep within you unconsciously knows something that you don't consciously know? That the wisdom in your *Soul* knows more than the self-focus in your *Head* does?

Our Egos Versus Our *Souls*

You are probably skeptically thinking, "What planet are you from? Don't you know that salespeople are mainly motivated by money?"

My answer is, of course most of us are motivated by money. First, we have to have it to pay our bills. We can do a lot of good things with money that we can't do without it. What I'm suggesting is the way to *earn more* money. It's here that all of us who sell must make decisions. We earn more by first focusing on creating the most value for the most people and then being paid accordingly.

There's nothing wrong with thinking about how we might earn more money. The question is in *how* we earn it. What focus causes us to earn the most? Which contributes to our highest sense of meaning? Professionalism? Client respect?

Clearly, it takes significant degrees of ego to choose to be a salesperson: risking and handling rejection, wondering what next month or next year will bring. Who of us doesn't need recognition, affirmation, and appreciation? Egos can spawn positive or negative energy.

They can be our friends or our enemies. Our values will determine our choices about where we focus this energy.

A Purpose Self-Assessment

Please read each statement and ask yourself, "How well does this statement describe me?" If it's very descriptive, circle 10; if it's not at all descriptive, circle 1; if it's somewhat descriptive, circle the appropriate number in between.

1. I mainly think about how much value I can create for people, knowing that I'll be compensated accordingly.

    1 2 3 4 5 6 7 8 9 10

2. I strongly believe that I should be highly compensated when I first create high value for people.

    1 2 3 4 5 6 7 8 9 10

3. My sincere client-focused purpose gives me high energy, self-confidence, and professionalism.

    1 2 3 4 5 6 7 8 9 10

4. My client-focused purpose greatly reduces any fear or call reluctance I might have.

    1 2 3 4 5 6 7 8 9 10

5. I mainly talk about the benefits my products or services will help clients enjoy, rather than just explaining the features they have.

    1 2 3 4 5 6 7 8 9 10

6. I have transitioned from product- or transaction-focused to client-focused selling.

1 2 3 4 5 6 7 8 9 10

7. I have a clear, written client-focused purpose statement that drives all my selling behaviors.

1 2 3 4 5 6 7 8 9 10

8. When people ask me what I do, I explain the benefits I help customers enjoy, not the products I sell.

1 2 3 4 5 6 7 8 9 10

9. I constantly analyze how I can help create more value for more people.

1 2 3 4 5 6 7 8 9 10

10. I set high goals for creating value for people, and I am confident that I will be highly compensated.

1 2 3 4 5 6 7 8 9 10

Total: _____

After finishing this self-assessment, go back and evaluate how your clients or customers might score you in each one. You might copy these ten statements, and ask your manager to score you. Think about sharing one or two of the statements with him or her, and ask for advice about how you might strengthen the traits.

What did you learn from this exercise?

How Your LifeStages Can
Influence Your Purpose

Let me introduce you to a model that can be of significant help in understanding where you are professionally, why you're reaching or not reaching performance goals, and what specific goals you need to set.

We all go through different LifeStages—times in our lives when circumstances or events beyond or within our control influence us mentally, emotionally, or spiritually. Some stages can displace us and block our productivity. Others can enhance it. Life is life. It isn't always good or bad. It can bring illness or good health. Financial disaster or abundance. Problems or blessings.

Take a few moments and study the following model:

Let's examine each of these stages:

1. Struggling
   a. Concerns—"I'm sinking fast and about to go under."
   b. Focus—almost totally on self and how one's life can be damaged.
   c. Motivation—to keep the worst from happening.
2. Coping
   a. Concerns—"I'm afraid of what's going to happen to me, and I must find a way to keep it from occurring."
   b. Focus—on negative consequences on self and loved ones.
   c. Motivation—fight or flight.

PROGRESSION OF LIFESTAGES

1 Struggling →	2 Coping →	3 Learning →	4 Stabilizing →	5 Succeeding →	6 Growing →	7 Evolving →
Fighting to preserve life: • Physically • Emotionally • Financially • Relationally	Totally defensive	Understanding causes	Regaining hope	Attaining productive goals	Making the most of one's life	Moving past material values
Survival mind-set	Faced with daily "fight or flight" decisions	Determining options	Setting productive goals	Feeling good about oneself	Learning for learning's sake	Desire to transcend humanness
Sees no place to turn	Dealing with fear, anxiety, or depression	Working toward solutions	Gaining confidence and profiting from bad experiences	Experiencing increased joy, peace, and thankfulness	Interest in "giving back"	Seeking higher wisdom and understanding
Little hope for the future	Energies, thoughts, actions focused on how to "get by"	Moving from panic to action	Developing resiliency and emotional tensile strength	Freedom from life's pressures	Seeking to understand own potential	Focusing on making the world a better place to live

3. Learning
   a. Concerns—"How can I find a way out and prevent the worst from happening again?"
   b. Focus—on understanding causes of problems and seeking solutions.
   c. Motivation—to move past pain and ease tensions.
4. Stabilizing
   a. Concerns—"I'm seeking stability and attempting to learn from the past so as not to make the same mistakes."
   b. Focus—on reducing risks or future problems and beginning to look ahead.
   c. Motivation—to build on a solid base.
5. Succeeding
   a. Concerns—"I'm doing pretty well and am focused on expanding my knowledge, skills, and successes."
   b. Focus—outward on expanding success and creating value for others.
   c. Motivation—to increase personal and professional success, build relationships, and discover new talents and abilities.
6. Growing
   a. Concerns—"All my material needs are being filled; I want to give my life to higher purposes."
   b. Focus—outward on creating value for others and enjoying the rewards of doing so.
   c. Motivation—to mine all inner spiritual resources and become all one can become.

7. Evolving

     a. Concerns—"I want to move past physical or material values and develop deeper spiritual understandings."

     b. Focus—totally off oneself and on the betterment of humankind.

     c. Motivation—to develop greater wisdom and understanding to help solve greater problems and contribute to the knowledge bank of the universe.

Points to Understand

1. Whatever LifeStages you're on, you're primarily concerned with satisfying those specific needs and blinded to higher or lower stages.

2. You can be at different stages simultaneously in different areas of your life, although areas with the lowest stages will usually dominate your thinking and demand greater attention.

3. When a LifeStages is satisfied, you'll automatically move to the next higher one in that part of your life.

4. Your goals will be unconsciously screened out unless they address your present LifeStages.

5. Your goals should be focused on satisfying your current stages, which will then automatically move you to the next higher one.

To help you understand and set goals that address your present LifeStages, the following learning process has been prepared for you to graphically plot where you are in different areas of your life.

Plotting Your LifeStages

For each category in the following chart, place a check mark in the appropriate column, with 1 being Struggling and 7 being Evolving:

	1	2	3	4	5	6	7
Financial							
Social							
Family							
Career							
Spiritual							
Personal Health							

Remember, the lower-numbered LifeStages will usually demand the most attention and will continue their silent pleadings until their needs are met. Attempting to reach higher goals in other areas of your life will meet unconscious resistance until the lower levels have been satisfied.

What areas of your life are on your two or three lowest levels? What goals do you need to set to satisfy those levels and move you to the next highest ones?

Setting Goals to Satisfy LifeStages

The secret of effective goal achievement is to define goals that will satisfy your current LifeStages. As you reach these goals, you automatically move up to higher ones and free up lower stages of your life that may have been sabotaging your ability to reach higher sales and life goals.

Please record your responses to these questions:

1. What areas of your life are at your two lowest LifeStages based on the preceding chart?
2. What actions can you take to satisfy each of them?

The lower these two stages are, the more they'll scream for attention. At this point you may not know exactly what actions to take to satisfy these two lower stages, but if you keep asking, you'll begin to receive answers.

Consider the Way You Set Sales and Income Goals

While we're on the subject of goal-setting, let me give you a quick preview of an effective process.

Many salespeople set goals like this:

1. Income I want to earn.
2. Sales I have to make to earn this income.
3. Activities I must do to sell this much.
4. What I'll do with the money I earn.

This is the process they're coached to use, and one that seems natural to them. May I offer a suggestion about rearranging the order of these goals?

1. Value I'll create for clients.
2. What I can do for them to create this value.
3. Sales I'll need to make to create this value.
4. Income I'll earn when I create this value.
5. Rewards I'll enjoy when I earn this income.

This process gives you total freedom to earn whatever you want to earn so you can enjoy the rewards you want to enjoy. Should you want to earn more, focus on how you can help your customers enjoy greater value. Both the client value you create and the resulting amount you earn will nurture your deep sense of worthiness in the recesses of your soul.

Please take a few moments and consider this five-step goal achievement process. Will it change the way you currently set goals? Will it change how you think, how you plan, and how you contact prospects or customers? Will it change your view of selling? Will it enhance the professional picture you have of yourself? Will it provide you with a more fulfilling sense of meaning to satisfy the silent call of your *Soul*?

Purpose Goals and Profit Goals

Daniel Pink, writing in his excellent book *Drive*, quotes several studies clearly showing that a "*purpose goal*" yields superior results than a "*profit goal*." He referred to a study done at the University of Rochester where students set both profit and purpose goals while still in school there. Pink then reported on their results a year later by writing about the students who had set profit goals:

> What's more, graduates with profit goals showed increases in anxiety, depression, and other negative indicators—again, even though they were attaining their goals.

He then contrasted these with students who'd set purpose goals:

> The people who had set purpose goals and felt they were attaining them reported higher levels of satisfaction and subjective

well-being than when they were in college, and quite low levels
of anxiety and depression.

The results are quite startling, aren't they?

Our observation of salespeople in the trenches of life, developing
client-focused selling, bears his conclusions out.

The Multiplying Power of Achievement Drive

Dr. David C. McClelland, professor of psychology at Harvard University, spent more than fifty years researching what he called *achievement drive*, or *need for achievement*. His basic belief was that achievement drive is the multiplier of all our other skills and abilities. It's the extent to which we desire to reach certain goals. The strength of our drive is evidenced by how long we'll work through roadblocks, challenges, and temporary defeats.

Consider the following sales power formula, which shows the multiplying effects of achievement drive:

    Product Knowledge
    + Sales Skills
    + Inherent Abilities
    + Selling Experience
    + Systems and Resources
    × Achievement Drive
    = Sales Power

You can release higher levels of achievement drive by doing the following:

- Setting specific goals that you feel a high desire to enjoy.
- Visualizing the rewards of reaching them.
- Associating with people who are achieving the levels of goals you want to reach.
- Setting up a supportive environment of people who encourage you.

Achievement Drive Self-Assessment

Please read each statement and ask yourself, "How well does this statement describe me?" If it's very descriptive, circle 10; if it's not at all descriptive, circle 1; if it's somewhat descriptive, circle the appropriate number in between.

1. People refer to me as being "highly motivated."

   1   2   3   4   5   6   7   8   9   10

2. I'm much more goal-oriented than process-oriented.

   1   2   3   4   5   6   7   8   9   10

3. I often fantasize about the rewards that reaching my goals will bring me.

   1   2   3   4   5   6   7   8   9   10

4. I'm always looking for new ways and ideas to reach higher goals.

   1   2   3   4   5   6   7   8   9   10

5. I view defeats, roadblocks, and challenges as temporary, and seek ways to move around them.

$$1 \quad 2 \quad 3 \quad 4 \quad 5 \quad 6 \quad 7 \quad 8 \quad 9 \quad 10$$

6. I am willing to take calculated risks; in fact, I thrive on them.

$$1 \quad 2 \quad 3 \quad 4 \quad 5 \quad 6 \quad 7 \quad 8 \quad 9 \quad 10$$

7. I'm constantly reading self-help books and listening to high achievers.

$$1 \quad 2 \quad 3 \quad 4 \quad 5 \quad 6 \quad 7 \quad 8 \quad 9 \quad 10$$

8. My need for achievement overpowers my fear of rejection.

$$1 \quad 2 \quad 3 \quad 4 \quad 5 \quad 6 \quad 7 \quad 8 \quad 9 \quad 10$$

9. I'm emotionally charged with a "high" when I make a sale.

$$1 \quad 2 \quad 3 \quad 4 \quad 5 \quad 6 \quad 7 \quad 8 \quad 9 \quad 10$$

10. I'm always picking the brains of successful people.

$$1 \quad 2 \quad 3 \quad 4 \quad 5 \quad 6 \quad 7 \quad 8 \quad 9 \quad 10$$

Total: _____

How to Benefit the Most from This Chapter

Remember, knowledge is not power until it's applied in constructive ways toward productive goals. By doing the following activities you'll benefit the most:

1. Read and review this chapter, marking up important points.

2. Meet with your study group and follow the instructions that you'll read in a moment.

3. Take the time to write out your own purpose statements for both your career and your personal life.

4. Review the Progression of LifeStages model.

   a. Check off what LifeStages you're on in the six parts of your life.

   b. Identify the areas of your life that are at the two lowest stages.

   c. Determine actions you can take to satisfy those stages, so you'll move to the next ones.

Performing these Action Steps will provide a foundation for significant growth and increased sales.

Keep your purpose statement handy; read it and say it to yourself several times each day. When the person in the mirror asks you, "Who are you, and what do you do?" look him or her in the eyes and repeat your purpose statement.

When someone asks you what you do, don't tell them what you sell; tell them the benefits you help clients enjoy.

Each time you repeat your purpose statement, you'll build your enthusiasm, confidence, and sense of purpose and meaning.

How to Accelerate Your Learning and Sales Success

Since the beliefs in your *I Am* only change experientially, let me share with you a small group study process that will greatly increase what you can gain from this book.

1. Select four or five other success-oriented salespeople and ask them to meet once each week for one hour.
2. Explain the purpose of the group:
   a. To spend a few weeks sharing success experiences they learned from the book.
   b. To increase their sales success.
   c. To be part of a growth group.
3. Each person in the group will need a copy of this book to study and report on each week.
4. Explain what you'll do in the meetings:
   a. Each person will read a chapter each week, apply the concepts, and report on their practice in the group sessions.
   b. Each person will share:
      i. What one action they chose to apply.
      ii. How they applied it.
      iii. What their results were.
      iv. What they learned.
   c. Keep all discussions on each person's practice, and off opinions, concepts, and ideology.
   d. Keep everything positive, avoiding arguments or disagreements.
5. After each person has shared these experiences, review them along with the lessons learned from the chapter:
   a. Look through the chapter and offer points they can practice.
   b. Share how they might practice the points.
   c. Share the results they might enjoy when they practice the points.
6. Vote for one group member who has best practiced an action.

Your commitment to these group meetings will significantly multiply the benefits you can gain from the book, as compared to just reading and applying the concepts. You'll learn from the others' experiences, as well as from their support and encouragement.

2

AUTHENTICITY

BRINGING YOUR KNOWLEDGE, EMOTIONS, AND VALUES INTO CONGRUENCE

*Don't aim for success—the more you aim at it and make
it a target, the more you are going to miss it. For success,
like happiness, cannot be pursued; it must ensue, and it only
does so as the unintended side-effect of one's personal
dedication to a cause greater than oneself.*

—VIKTOR FRANKL, MD

Be careful what you aim for, as you may hit it.

Did Dr. Frankl really know what he was talking about when he wrote this? Isn't it good to *aim* for success? To make it a *target*? To *pursue* it? To set success goals? What's wrong with that?

Or could it be that in his wisdom he understood that success and happiness are *serendipitous*—coming into our lives by process of indirection? That to enjoy them, we must first seek something else? Then, as an unintended consequence, we enjoy true success and happiness? Could it be that true success does *ensue* as a side effect of our career purpose:

- First, to create the most value for the most people?
- Second, to be rewarded consistently with the value we create?

How many of us daily wrestle with a void in our lives that's caused by an unanswered and maybe misdirected search for meaning? With the emotional ups and downs of selling, our purpose can lead us to fulfillment or despair.

Is it possible for us to have several strong habits or skills, and yet some deep belief boundaries or conflicts can block us and emotionally torpedo us in different degrees? This happened on a tragic level for a good friend of mine, as I briefly mentioned in the Introduction.

Dave Golden was the regional managing director of the Principal Financial Group's Colorado region. For years he enjoyed a moderate level of success, until his career caught fire and his business began to really take off.

He'd just been certified to conduct one of my courses, and he told me how excited he was about doing it for his agents. He admitted that he had "been in a funk for several months," and that this would help bring him out. He conducted the course, and his business began to climb upward.

One day he called me and told me he had set a goal to build a new home in Denver and wanted to know if he could send me a picture of it. Of course I said yes.

As the months went by, he called and told me that his new home would be finished on a certain date and asked me to come and be his family's first dinner guest. So I went and conducted a sales meeting for his agency and then had dinner in his beautiful two-story home. It seemed such a happy occasion. Dave, his beautiful wife and children, and I enjoyed a wonderful dinner.

What an inspiring storybook success experience. Goals, hard work, dedication, fine family.

It was only a few weeks later when I got a call that he had gone into the men's room of an adjacent office building, with nothing in his pocket but a calling card, put a gun to his temple, and pulled the trigger.

Everyone who knew him was completely shocked. Why did he do that? How could the gap between his external success and his internal struggles have been so wide and well hidden?

Three times during the year before his death, he called me and asked to come to Phoenix, spend the afternoon with me, and have dinner. Each time he told me two stories several times that might shed some light on his inner turmoil.

When Dave was growing up, his father drove an old dilapidated truck, picking up rags, junk, or any scrap metal. One day his father pulled the truck in front of a malt shop that kids he knew frequented. They were dirty and sweaty, and his father gave him some money and told him to go in and bring out two malts.

Slumping down in the truck so his friends wouldn't see him, he refused to go in. His father gave him a stiff verbal reaming out, went in himself, and brought out one malt; he sat in the truck drinking it and continuing his very stern lecture about Dave's behavior.

After Dave was grown and earning a very nice income, he bought a lifelong dream car—a Porsche. He called his father to tell him about the new car, hoping to hear words of praise and approval. Unfortunately, that wasn't what he received. His father asked him how much it cost. When Dave told him, his father exploded, screaming several reasons why he didn't deserve to have anything that cost that much and why he shouldn't keep it, demanding that he take it back.

Rather than feeling a sense of accomplishment and having his father thrilled at his success, Dave was deeply emotionally shattered.

Each time he told me this story, he'd look at me with deep hurt in his eyes and say, "And . . . I took it back!" He'd painfully pause and then say, "It was as if I had no resistance to my father's demands. Ever since then I've wanted to buy another one, and even though I can afford it, I can never bring myself to do it."

"You Don't Deserve It"

Throughout his upbringing, Dave's script was firmly set in invisible ink: "You don't deserve it." His high achievement drive drove him to prove he could be successful. All the while, his desire to prove his father wrong butted heads with the old scripts that had been indelibly written in his *I Am*, resulting in conflict, pain, anger, confusion, and inner disharmony. Gigantic clashes between wanting to prove his father wrong and wanting his father's approval reached a flash point of internal combustion where he could no longer handle it.

An Unusual Story?

My friend's story is unusual in scope and outcome but not in principle. Graduates from our courses tell me over and over how life events—both positive and negative ones—have caused them to assume certain self-beliefs and then perform consistently with these accepted "truths."

But in many cases, these accepted "truths" are not truth at all, only fabrications.

Martin E. P. Seligman, PhD, writing in his excellent book, *Learned Optimism*, suggests, "Usually, the negative beliefs that follow adversity are inaccurate." It's when our emotional and spiritual immune systems are challenged that we are at our weakest. In this condition it's natural to allow negative evaluations to creep through the sometimes thin walls of our belief systems.

Why and where does all this happen within us? What can we do about old limiting belief boundaries? And what do we have to do to develop strong, successful beliefs that drive positive sales activities and resulting success?

Let's think more deeply about the levels of consciousness that are constantly at work within you.

The Three Levels of Consciousness

I quickly shared this model in the introduction and will be referring to it several times throughout this book, as it helps illustrate the central theme of the book. I've explained it hundreds of times to audiences, and every time I do, I learn more about it. It's a framework, or matrix, to better understand the deeper issues that are driving your sales behaviors. Since our *I Am* contains the spiritual, infinite intelligence, or spirit of truth within us, we can continue to learn more, but never saturating the learning possibilities. These four points will help you begin to understand some of the power involved:

1. How powerful your emotions are in motivating your activities and behavior.
2. How your rational knowledge interacts with your deeper unconscious values, your belief boundaries, and the spirit of truth to produce your behaviors.
3. What kinds of choices cause strong positive energy and confidence.
4. How your view of selling interacts with the values in your unconscious *I Am*.

THE THREE LEVELS OF CONSCIOUSNESS
Behaviors

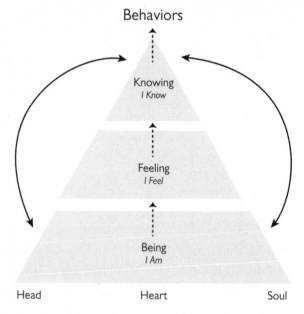

Let's simplify our profoundly complex knowledge/emotional/ spiritual psyche—the whole of which defies description. This model helps us understand the interactions within us that need to be balanced in order to change behavior. All three of these levels of consciousness work together to create our behaviors.

Your *I Know* is your logical, fully conscious, intellectual level— the *Head*. With it you make decisions, exercise choices, and learn information. Most of your formal education was directed to this part of you, as is most training today. While it is important to continually gain knowledge and information, most of what you hear, read, or learn is consciously forgotten within a few days and handed off into your unconscious storage, where it is available but hardly ever accessed.

While knowledge is necessary, it takes more than that for successful living and selling. Much of the so-called training many salespeople get today is only product and application education. The assumption is that if salespeople know their products, they'll go sell them. But although it's necessary, successful selling takes much more than mere knowledge.

It's amazing how some very intelligent senior executives with big companies don't know this.

Psychologist Price Pritchett conducted one of my courses years ago as the basis for his PhD dissertation. He gathered forty-five agents from three agencies with one of the "big three" life insurance companies headquartered in New York City. Price split them up into three groups of fifteen, gave them five psychological assessments that only licensed psychologists could use, and compiled their manager evaluations and sales numbers for the last six months. These same numbers were gathered twelve weeks later and compared.

One group took our then-nine-week DynaGroup personal growth course, meeting weekly. The second group was given audio messages from the weekly course material to listen to, but they did not attend weekly sessions. The third group was a pure control group that didn't attend sessions or listen to audio messages. During the twelve weeks after the experiment ended, there was less than 1 percent difference in the sales of the control group and the audiocassette group. But the group that went through the course had almost a 50 percent increase in sales over the other two groups.

When we got the results, we were sure that the company would give us 51 percent of their company just for implementing the course throughout the United States. We got an appointment with the head of agencies in New York. After we introduced ourselves and shared our purpose, he became almost livid, wanting to know who authorized our project. Price told him the three agency managers did, and he wrote their names down.

After a few minutes of not listening to us, this senior executive interrupted and said, "Well, we don't need any of this motivational stuff. We give our agents plenty of product knowledge, and we think if they know their products, they'll go out and sell them."

Where had this man been hibernating? Certainly not in the real world.

As a tribute to this man's wisdom and leadership, a couple of years later this company lost their leadership positions to a competitor.

Price and I crept out of this man's office, took the elevator down to the street, had dinner, licked our wounds, and assessed our bombed sales call, finally realizing that our Mediterranean yacht purchase would have to be delayed a bit. And the chain of banks we were going to buy when we closed this deal would probably have to wait for a while.

Well, my point, again, is that while knowledge is necessary for sales success, it only gets us into the arena but doesn't win games. There are more powerful forces within us that cause us to win at the selling game. Yet today, most sales training is merely dispensing information. The assumption is that salespeople will hear, understand, remember, and apply. But around 95 percent of this never finds its way into your actions.

Our Emotions Often Trump Our Knowledge

Your *I Know*, your *Head*, has certain limitations of power when compared to your *I Feel*, your *Heart*. Consider that in your day-to-day selling your *I Feel*, or your emotions, will trump your product knowledge, systems, and processes around 85 percent of the time.

Have you ever driven around and around the block on the way to a sales call, hoping you wouldn't find a parking spot? Because if you did, you'd have to go up on the twenty-fifth floor and call on that purchasing agent who emotionally stripped you of any sense of self-confidence the last time you met?

Since selling is largely an emotional game, not a logical one, the influence of emotions creates lots of problems for both salespeople and managers. Managers or trainers can teach the necessary knowledge but generally sidestep the emotional part and dismiss it as "soft skills."

Think for a moment about how your emotions silently speak to you, and drive so many of your behaviors. Like: "I know I shouldn't argue so much with Cletus, my brother-in-law, but he's such a smart-mouth, and everything he says drives me up the wall. I wonder what my sister ever saw in him. Sometimes I just have to set him straight. If he'd just follow my advice and example more, I wouldn't get so ticked off at him. It's all his fault."

Or, "I just don't know how to handle the anxiety I have when I lose a big sale. I tend to get emotionally down and wonder if I'll be able to make it financially."

Or, "Every time I pick up the phone to try to get an appointment with someone I perceive to be more important than I am, my arm seems to freeze up and my stomach does flip-flops."

Think of all the times when your emotions fueled huge amounts of positive energy, and you were unstoppable. Or the other times when you lost three sales in a row, and you weren't sure you'd ever make another one. Emotional control becomes a vital discipline in the sales field.

Here's where rewards can help us develop resistance to emotional threats.

Not to brag or anything like that, but I've discovered a way to handle the different emotions I experience. When I've worked hard, had a very good week, and am feeling great, I *reward* myself by going to an In-N-Out Burger for lunch on Saturday. A full deal—Double-Double and fries. Having this weekly *reward* motivates me and causes me to feel unconquerable. On the other hand, when I've had a really difficult week and catch myself starting to feel down, I *encourage* myself by going to an In-N-Out Burger for lunch on Saturday. This weekly *encouragement* causes me to feel unconquerable, lifting me out of any physical, emotional, or spiritual lows.

Well, maybe you have more refined tastes than I do, so rent a Porsche and go to Ruth's Chris Steak House to reward or encourage yourself.

Whatever causes you to feel unconquerable.

Our *I Am* Plays a Major Role

Your *I Am*, your *Soul*, is the creative unconscious part within you. It houses the emotional thermostat that controls your values, moral codes, inner belief boundaries, creative mechanism, sense of worthiness, life force, intuition, and instincts. It's infused with Dr. Carl Jung's *spirit of truth*. This is the part of you that's been created in the image of God.

Far below our conscious thinking level, this spirit of truth communicates with others through intuitive powers of which most people have little understanding. We use terms such as *intuition*, *rapport*, *empathy*, or *sixth sense* to explain this connection with others.

Being our spiritual dimension, your *Soul* hatches dreams and floats creative ideas by us from time to time. It triggers emotions of guilt, remorse, anger, love, joy, peace, and happiness. It comes hardwired to help us enjoy positive emotions as a result of the value we create for others. We experience negative emotions when our choices, decisions, or actions conflict with truth, honor, and justice.

The interaction of these three consciousness levels—*Head*, *Heart*, and *Soul*—creates our emotions and works together to cause many of our decisions and automatic behaviors.

Let's think about how this happens.

The Interaction of the Three Levels of Consciousness

During your waking hours your conscious *I Know* is continually interacting with your unconscious *I Am*. The nature of the interaction triggers an emotion in your *I Feel*. In turn, your emotions are so strong that they can trump or support the thoughts, decisions, or logic in your *I Know*.

Please stop and meditate on this for a few moments. Almost all of your decisions or actions go through this process: Your *I Know* connects with your *I Am*, then triggers consistent emotions in your *I Feel*, which supports or overrules the decisions in your *I Know*.

You can dissect almost all your decisions and actions by identifying your thoughts, decisions, and actions generated by your *I Know*, and how they interact with your values, belief boundaries, and spirit of truth in your *I Am*.

For example:

> I know that I should call and get an appointment with a senior decision maker, but I've been rebuffed by her assistant, and I don't want to go through that again, so I'll wait until tomorrow, when I get my confidence pumped up.

Have you ever gone through a similar experience? Most of us have. Please hang with me. Here's what was taking place within you.

Your *I Know* was aware that you needed to make the call, but the lingering memories of old personal hurts in your *I Am* say, "*I don't want to experience that same rejection again.*" So your *I Feel* overrules your *I Know*, and you put off contacting that person, hoping you'll feel more confident tomorrow.

It's this type of interaction that causes call reluctance or fear of rejection, which then kills many salespeople's productivity.

Or the opposite can happen.

For example:

> I know that I may be able to help this organization increase their efficiency and overall productivity. Although I was rebuffed by the decision maker's assistant once, I owe it to them to talk to the decision maker to see if I can help them. So it's not about my being accepted or rejected by her assistant, it's really about finding out if they want or need my help.

By changing our view of selling, and emotionally accepting that new construct, we can counteract negative emotional blocks that have hampered our activity levels.

This may be a bit confusing now, but as you go through this book, you'll learn more about making decisions that give you greater emotional control. As this happens, your life changes.

Selling Success Is a Matter of Harmony of the Three Levels

Sales success is a matter of bringing the thoughts, decisions, and knowledge of your *I Know* into harmony with the beliefs, values, spirit of truth, and hardwiring within your *I Am*. When your values are client-focused and you consciously choose to practice the CLIENT-Focused Sales System that you'll learn in the next chapter, positive emotions are triggered that support and give energy to your decisions. The resulting actions then cause you to have more confidence and increased activity levels.

Dr. Carl Jung calls this harmonic activity a *transcendent function*, or "the union of conscious and unconscious contents." In simple language it means to make choices in our *I Know* that are congruent with the beliefs, values, or moral code in our *I Am*. This is a nonspecific transcendent function for you—moving you past where you currently are. It's working on the causes, rather than on the effects.

What's this got to do with selling?

Everything. For instance, when your conscious choice to practice client-focused selling is in harmony with the hardwired values in your *I Am*, positive emotions are triggered in your emotional *I Feel* that energize and empower you.

Since selling is an inner (mental) game, 85 percent of your success will be influenced by the programming in your *I Am*, your *Soul*. As this transcendent function, or the integration of the Three Levels of Consciousness, takes place within you, your emotional and spiritual forces work together to empower you.

You've never heard this in any sales training you've experienced, have you? So much of this book is directed toward helping you carry out the previous paragraph.

Sales Power Congruence Model

Let's think of some factors that, when they are in harmony, tend to create a synchronicity between your *Head*, *Heart*, and *Soul*. This causes you to generate energy, confidence, and increased productivity.

As you learned in Chapter 1, your purpose is your intent, your motivation, or your reason for selling. It becomes the *why* you sell, and the *why* drives the *how* you sell. To ensure the highest productive outcome, your purpose must be:

1. to create the most value for the most people, and
2. to thankfully receive the compensation that's consistent with the value you create.

THE SALES POWER CONGRUENCE MODEL

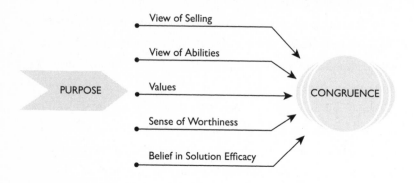

This balanced purpose—the cause—will then drive successful attitudes, values, and behaviors, influencing how and what you sell—the effects. Higher levels of success will occur when these elements flow together without conflicts to jam their gears. A client-focused purpose will drive consistent behaviors, thinking patterns, and self-beliefs.

When your choices and actions are in harmony with the spirit of truth in your *I Am*, you'll begin to access emotional powers that can multiply the effectiveness of your knowledge and abilities. As this inner *synergistic* power builds, the whole becomes greater than the sum of your individual abilities. You'll access new energies that will transcend logical explanation.

I'm fascinated with this concept of *synergy*—the whole becoming greater than the sum of its parts. It applies to the congruence model just mentioned, as well as to a team that becomes greater than the sum of its players' abilities.

I read a story once about the early days of California. In Death Valley, hearty wagoneers hauled the mineral borax out of pits to a rail station a few miles away. For a long time each wagon was pulled by twelve mules. A creative thinker, tinkering around, discovered that adding eight mules to the team enabled it to pull two wagons plus a water wagon. Adding eight to twelve more than doubled the pulling capacity.

This is where the term for the product *20 Mule Team Borax* came from. The next time you're in a supermarket, pick out this detergent. You'll see the picture of twenty mules pulling two huge wagons plus a water wagon behind.

Another example of synergy—the whole becoming greater than the sum of its parts—took place back in the early days of building and testing rockets. Back then a C-1 missile was composed of eight Redstone rockets. But the measured thrust of a C-1 missile was 24 times the thrust of one Redstone rocket—meaning that in synergistic measurements, the combination tripled the thrust of the eight rockets.

Like the sums of these physical powers being multiplied, so your emotional powers increase when your purpose is in sync with the factors of the preceding congruence model.

A Purpose Self-Assessment

Although you scored yourself in a longer assessment in the last chapter, please take a moment and read each of the following statements. Ask yourself, "How descriptive is this statement of my actual selling behaviors?" If it's always descriptive, circle 10; if it's never descriptive, circle 1; if it's sometimes descriptive, circle the appropriate number in between.

1. I have a clear, written purpose statement that drives my behaviors.

$$1 \quad 2 \quad 3 \quad 4 \quad 5 \quad 6 \quad 7 \quad 8 \quad 9 \quad 10$$

2. My client focus greatly reduces any fear or call reluctance I have.

1 2 3 4 5 6 7 8 9 10

3. I am much more client-focused than product- or transaction-focused.

1 2 3 4 5 6 7 8 9 10

4. To earn more, I know I must create more value for customers.

1 2 3 4 5 6 7 8 9 10

5. The more value I create for my customers, the better I feel about myself.

1 2 3 4 5 6 7 8 9 10

Total: _____

Looking back at these statements, on which one did you score yourself the highest? On which one did you score the lowest? Using this assessment, determine a couple of actions you might take to improve your lowest scores.

Remember, your true driving purpose will influence your attitudes, your actions, and their resulting sales and compensation. A client focus will become a foundation for allowing positive, synergistic powers to develop within you. Other focuses often negate your natural powers.

Now, let's think about each of the factors in the congruence model.

View of Selling

Your view of selling is how you define the process. Is it doing things *for* people, or getting people to do things *for you*? Is it creating the most value for yourself, or creating the most value for clients, content that you'll be compensated consistently with the value you create?

I previously mentioned John Cato, who had graduated from my Authentic Salesperson Course. He has called me several times since graduating, telling me how practicing the CLIENT-Focused Sales System has completely changed his view of selling, but mainly his results. Before he took the course, his purpose was to close as much business as he could so he could earn as much money and win as many contests as possible. His driving purpose was to create value for himself. But much of the business he wrote got canceled within a few months—because it really wasn't sold to begin with.

It took him a while to transition from his old income- or transaction-focused selling style to a true client focus. He experienced conflicts and doubt that the change would really work for him. This is normal, as most changes cause some stress. He'd previously enjoyed a nice income and was afraid that it would drop if he changed his hard closing focus. At first, focusing on creating the most value for clients felt "out of sync," as he had to move past his old self-focused habits and sales patterns.

The reason for two or three of his calls was to tell me that he'd just made large sales. Rather than going as quickly to the close as he used to do, he spent extra time developing rapport and creating strong relationships with decision makers. He carefully asked questions to determine the current and desired situations of the client. His genuine desire was to create the most value for the client's company. He got the business over a well-known firm that had controlled the account for several years. His commission was just over $200,000 for this one sale. Another was $300,000.

He said, "I would never have gotten the account had I not followed your client-focused system."

His business changed when his view of selling came into alignment with his view of his abilities; both were congruent with strong, positive, ethical values.

View of Selling Self-Assessment

Please read each statement and ask yourself, "How well does this statement describe me?" If it's very descriptive, circle 10; if it's not at all descriptive, circle 1; if it's somewhat descriptive, circle the appropriate number in between.

1. I believe selling is first creating the most value for the most people, and then thankfully receiving compensation that's consistent with the value I create.

    1   2   3   4   5   6   7   8   9   10

2. I recommend my product or service only after I've gained rapport, thoroughly understood people's wants or needs, and believe my solutions will give clients the benefits they want to enjoy.

    1   2   3   4   5   6   7   8   9   10

3. I believe selling is helping people, rather than getting them to help me.

    1   2   3   4   5   6   7   8   9   10

4. I believe selling is a win-win partnering with clients to help them enjoy benefits they wouldn't otherwise experience.

1 2 3 4 5 6 7 8 9 10

5. I always focus on how much I can help people, knowing that my compensation will come.

1 2 3 4 5 6 7 8 9 10

Total: _____

What did you learn from scoring yourself on this assessment?

View of Abilities

Your view of abilities is your answer to the question: "Do you believe you possess the ability to do what you think selling is?" When your answer is *no*, a deep conflict within your emotional and spiritual dimensions will occur. It'll block your ability to sell on higher levels.

This conflict may result because you have a distorted view of what selling is. Frankly, most salespeople do. Do you view it as a professional process of helping people receive value they wouldn't otherwise enjoy, if it weren't for your help? Or do you see it as a process of persuading people to buy from you? Some people still think selling is for superheroes, people who have blue suits and red capes with a big *S* on them.

Not so, amigo.

A wrong view of selling may be the biggest killer of sales success, claiming more careers than almost any other factor. To the extent that your view of selling is persuading people to buy what you're selling, you'll meet emotional conflict after conflict. This is why old "closing techniques" and "overcoming stalls and objections" strategies were so destructive to the moral fiber of salespeople.

As I've trained, listened to, and received letters and emails from many salespeople, I believe the conflict between their view of selling, and their view of their abilities, sabotages more of them than almost anything else.

Along with the new definition of selling that I've shared with you, the CLIENT-Focused Sales System that you'll learn in Chapters 3 through 9 gives you a step-by-step process that will improve your view of your abilities.

When you understand the system, you'll gain the confidence to practice it. When you begin to practice it, you'll find that customers are attracted to you and want to do business with you. You'll find it to be self-rewarding—and your customers will feel good about doing business with you.

View of Abilities Self-Assessment

Please read each statement and ask yourself, "How well does this statement describe me?" If it's very descriptive, circle 10; if it's not at all descriptive, circle 1; if it's somewhat descriptive, circle the appropriate number in between.

1. I never doubt my abilities to be successful in selling.

   1 2 3 4 5 6 7 8 9 10

2. If selling is helping people, rather than persuading them to buy from me, I believe I can do that.

   1 2 3 4 5 6 7 8 9 10

3. I have a strong eagerness to learn and to expand my skills and abilities.

   1 2 3 4 5 6 7 8 9 10

4. Doing things that help people is congruent with my values and is demonstrated in other parts of my life.

   1 2 3 4 5 6 7 8 9 10

5. My own interests as well as my friends tell me that I'm very good in dealing with people.

   1 2 3 4 5 6 7 8 9 10

   Total: _____

How did your responses here coordinate with your view of selling? Any conflicts? How might either of these be influencing your sales success?

Values

Values are the personal rules by which we live our lives. They become guidelines directing how we'll make decisions and respond to different life situations or challenges. Here are some fundamental selling values that give substance to our decisions, actions, and quality of life.

- I do the right thing because it's the right thing to do.
- I desire to help as many people as I can.
- I enjoy contacting people, and they appreciate my desire to help them.

- I go the extra mile and give customers more than they expect of me.
- I focus on understanding and fulfilling the needs of customers, and when I do my own needs are met.
- I tell the truth in all situations, unless it would hurt someone.
- I do unto others as I would want them to do unto me.
- I know I'll enjoy high levels of prosperity when I create high value for others.

You'll notice that I've stated these as affirmations, or self-suggestions, so you can repeat them to yourself several times each day. This practice, with repetition and visualization of how you can apply them, will program them into your *I Am*. After this programming, you'll perform them unconsciously.

Whenever situations occur in which you need to be guided by one of these value affirmations, your unconscious *I Am* will send a message through your *I Feel* to your conscious *I Know*. For instance, suppose you're having a bit of call reluctance, afraid you'll not be accepted by a buyer. When you experience this emotion, say to yourself, "I enjoy contacting people, and they appreciate my desire to help them." In fact, repeat it over and over to yourself.

While just saying this may not trigger your actions the first few times you say it, continued self-suggestions will eventually build an inner belief that will then send positive messages to you when you need them. So when a belief is built by repetition, and you experience some degree of fear of rejection, your *I Am* will send a message through your *I Feel* that says to your *I Know*, "Wait a minute . . . You enjoy contacting people, and they appreciate your desire to help them."

To help cement these inner beliefs, whenever you repeat your self-suggestions, stop a moment and visualize the rewards of practicing them. Mentally picture yourself doing them with your customers, and see your customers responding in positive, appreciative ways.

Values Self-Assessment

Please read each statement and ask yourself, "How well does this statement describe me?" If it's very descriptive, circle 10; if it's not at all descriptive, circle 1; if it's somewhat descriptive, circle the appropriate number in between.

1. I always do the right thing when it's the right thing to do.

   1 2 3 4 5 6 7 8 9 10

2. I always go the extra mile in all my relationships and transactions.

   1 2 3 4 5 6 7 8 9 10

3. I always tell the truth in all situations, unless it would hurt someone.

   1 2 3 4 5 6 7 8 9 10

4. I always do unto others as I would want them to do unto me.

   1 2 3 4 5 6 7 8 9 10

5. I always choose to have a positive regard for the rights of others.

   1 2 3 4 5 6 7 8 9 10

   Total: _____

What did you learn from this scoring? How might embracing and practicing these values influence your sales?

Sense of Worthiness

Our inner sense of worthiness defines what we deeply believe we deserve to have in life rewards. It has been formed by our responses to our life experiences. Without consciously realizing it, all of us make decisions about how good we are and what we should enjoy in life rewards.

We tend to buy into what other people tell us about ourselves. If we had parents, teachers, or other caring people who emotionally nourished or encouraged us, chances are we grew up with a positive view of ourselves and our possibilities for success. Conversely, a lack of support or love and frequent criticism can result in a negative opinion of our own worth and abilities. Then, whether our self-observations are right or wrong, we act accordingly. Our developed inner beliefs become self-fulfilling prophecies. After a while we quit questioning their authenticity and acquiesce to their control.

I can't remember a single time my father ever complimented me or encouraged me in even the slightest manner. Everything was a put-down, criticism, or anger vented toward me. The message was always clear: "You don't deserve to amount to much because you don't do anything right." I bought into a lot of what my father said *to* me and *about* me. It's taken years to work through a lot of that old programming. I suppose, though, that we don't live enough years to completely wash all that stuff out of our *I Am* dimensions.

But every adversity can be converted into blessings—if we choose to do so. Rather than harboring emotional and spiritual acid indigestion about past abuse I experienced from my father, I often give thanks for the results of it. I doubt that I would've been drawn to this wonderful business of building people's confidence had I not struggled to maintain a positive sense of self while growing up. It wasn't until I started conducting personal growth courses that I began to allow myself to understand my father's influence on my own opinion of my self-worth. I was learning, along with the course participants, to forgive past hurts and be thankful for the lessons they taught us.

I've learned that developing a stronger sense of worthiness is paradoxical—our *Heads* and *Hearts* may think one thing, but our *Souls* may know differently. Our *egos* may tell us that possessions, money, acclaim, or fame promise to give our lives meaning; but then we get them and discover that they sometimes fail to deliver. Our *Souls* know that it's first the value we create, and then our thankful acceptance of the resulting compensation or rewards we receive, that builds our sense of worthiness.

Sense of Worthiness Self-Assessment

Please read each statement and ask yourself, "How well does this statement describe me?" If it's very descriptive, circle 10; if it's not at all descriptive, circle 1; if it's somewhat descriptive, circle the appropriate number in between.

1. I strongly believe that I deserve to enjoy a high level of prosperity, because of the high value I help people enjoy.

   1   2   3   4   5   6   7   8   9   10

2. When I was growing up, my parents and teachers encouraged me to feel that I could achieve anything I wanted.

   1   2   3   4   5   6   7   8   9   10

3. I feel loved because I have strong, healthy, loving relationships in all areas of my life.

   1 2 3 4 5 6 7 8 9 10

4. It's easy for me to forgive others and solicit their forgiveness of me.

   1 2 3 4 5 6 7 8 9 10

5. I always go the extra mile and always give clients more than they pay me.

   1 2 3 4 5 6 7 8 9 10

Total: _____

Which of these statements would you most like to strengthen? What actions might you take to do so?

Belief in Solution Efficacy

Our prosperity expands to the degree to which we believe our products or services are more valuable to our clients than the money they pay us for them. When we sincerely believe this, we have stronger self-confidence, our fear of rejection vanishes, and our contact activity increases.

Several things happen when this increased value occurs for our customers:

- We become more valuable to them.
- We make it difficult for competitors to take our business away.
- We make it possible to earn more pay.

- We build an abundance mentality.
- We earn the respect of customers, which washes back to us as more self-respect.
- Our clients become our best salespeople.

Writing in his classic book *The Master Key to Riches*, Napoleon Hill penned this:

An important principle of success in all walks of life and in all occupations is a willingness to GO THE EXTRA MILE; which means the rendering of more and better service than that for which one is paid, and giving it in a *positive mental attitude*.

He then points out that this law is paradoxical

because *it is impossible for anyone to render such service without receiving appropriate compensation.*

Hill goes on to make his final point that there are two forms of compensation that come to us:

The compensation we receive in money, and
The skill, experience, wisdom, respect, reputation, or sense of worthiness we attain from the act.

Granted, these values are not always easy to understand for people who are dealing with survival levels in some aspect of their lives. I certainly understand the defeating effects of this Struggling level. I've been there. But unless we can recognize where we stand and what our future will be should we not alter our thinking and acting, we're destined to repeat the decisions that got us there.

Belief in Solution Efficacy Self-Assessment

Please read each statement and ask yourself, "How well does this statement describe me?" If it's very descriptive, circle 10; if it's not at all descriptive, circle 1; if it's somewhat descriptive, circle the appropriate number in between.

1. I always try to give customers more value than what they pay me for.

    1 2 3 4 5 6 7 8 9 10

2. I sincerely believe that my products/services give customers more value than our competitors can give them.

    1 2 3 4 5 6 7 8 9 10

3. I always focus on giving clients extra value beyond just the benefits my products/services provide them.

    1 2 3 4 5 6 7 8 9 10

4. In addition to talking about the features and benefits that my products/services provide my customers, I also emphasize the quality-of-life issues they might enjoy.

    1 2 3 4 5 6 7 8 9 10

5. I always try to understand each person who's involved in a sale and how they might personally benefit from the purchase.

    1 2 3 4 5 6 7 8 9 10

   Total: _____

Your belief in the efficacy of your products or services not only will influence your authenticity as you present them but will be unconsciously communicated to your customers. If customers don't feel you have total belief in your product efficacy, they will not believe you or have total confidence in you. Here's the question for you: "If you wouldn't buy what you're selling, why should a customer buy it?"

What did you learn by doing these assessments? What are your strengths? What areas need some improvement?

Let's delve deeper into what drives our success and productivity.

Congruence of Previous Factors

An intellectual, emotional, and spiritual congruence occurs when you can say you believe and practice the following statements:

1. *Purpose:* My purpose is to create the most value for the most people and to be compensated accordingly.
2. *View of Selling:* I believe selling is seeing as many people as possible to see who wants or needs my help. If they want or need my help, I help them. If they neither want nor need my help, I haven't failed; I've succeeded in finding out who needs my help.
3. *View of Abilities:* I believe I have the abilities to do what I think selling is.
4. *Values:* I allow strong, positive values to guide my selling behaviors.
5. *Sense of Worthiness:* I am worthy of enjoying high sales success, because I first focus on creating high value for clients.
6. *Belief in Solution Efficacy:* I believe my products or services create client value far beyond their cost.

When you can proclaim these values with true belief, you'll begin to build deep feelings of congruence, harmony, or consistency within your *I Am*.

As this transformation happens, you'll experience new levels of confidence. Passion for what you do. Respect for who you are. Affirmation of the value you create for others. Validation for your message.

All contributors to your genuine success.

"But," you ask, "where within me is all this happening?"

Your *I Am* Contains Your Inner Area-of-the-Possible

Consider the following model:

AREA-OF-THE-POSSIBLE

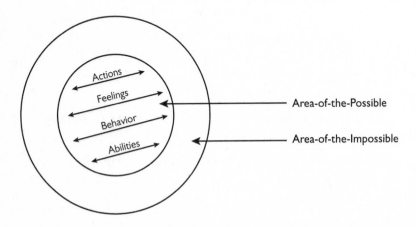

Securely housed inside your *I Am* resides your self-developed *area-of-the-possible*. This inner mechanism continually surveys all your past life experiences and evaluates how well you performed and your level of self-worth. These unconscious evaluations, along with your actual past sales, form your *area-of-the-possible*.

This is the inner voice of your *I Am* controlling what you believe to be possible or impossible for you to sell, gain, attain, or become. The voice isn't in a recognizable language like English, Spanish, or French. Rather it's in the form of *Soul* talk—silent voices coming from deep within your *I Am*. Fear. Confidence. Anxiety. Anticipation. Contact avoidance. Hope. Low or high energy. Achievement drive. Fear of rejection. Ups. Downs. Level of expectations. Degree of poverty or prosperity consciousness.

This inner belief boundary is so powerful that it will allow and then control most of your actions, feelings, behavior, and abilities, to the point at which you reach only those goals you believe to be within your possibilities. When we get close to the outer edges of this boundary, we tend to shut down as if it's impenetrable. All of us do this to different degrees.

Most people underevaluate their actual abilities and possibilities. Human nature seems to dwell on a handful of mistakes and defeats and ignore boatloads of successes, abilities, and noble acts. After listening to thousands of people in my courses, I'm convinced that the average person's negative beliefs outweigh their positive ones at least four to one.

Here's the point: Until your *area-of-the-possible* expands, your actions, feelings, behavior, and abilities—your *productivity*—will stay pretty much the same as it is now. Add to this the reality that most of us have continual outside negative pressure that can shrink our *area-of-the-possible*, should we allow it to happen.

I must emphasize that your *area-of-the-possible* isn't changed *intellectually*. Knowing that you have one has no power to change it either. It changes only *experientially*—by taking action and applying positive, client-focused activities over a period of time—which I'll have you doing in the rest of this book.

You Should Be Highly Compensated

If, after learning and practicing the CLIENT-Focused Sales System, you're not earning increased rewards, it may be a clear sign that your purpose is still not a true client focus or that you have conflict between one or more of the elements of the Sales Power Congruence Model:

- View of Selling
- View of Abilities
- Values
- Sense of Worthiness
- Belief in Solution Efficacy

From time to time, it's productive to go back and reassess ourselves in these areas. Since none of us is perfect, we're not going to perform all of these valuable behaviors perfectly. We must accept the fact that we're each under constant reconstruction.

But remember this: You should be highly paid. You should earn a lot of money or other forms of compensation—tangible or intangible—under the following conditions:

1. Your primary purpose is to create the most value for the most people.
2. You believe you should be compensated consistently with the value you create.
3. Your intention is to create high value for your customers.

How to Benefit the Most from This Chapter

You learned in this chapter that your sales are being influenced by internal beliefs that you've developed over your lifetime. We all develop compelling beliefs about who we are and what we're capable of achieving. Then, whether these beliefs are true or false, we live them out as if they were true, never questioning their authenticity.

I presented to you a Sales Power Congruence Model, detailing six success factors, from purpose to belief in solution efficacy, that can be congruent or conflicted. Please take some time this week and score yourself on each of them. After doing this, select two or three of the statements that you'd most like to strengthen the coming week.

1. Write them on an index card or your electronic device.
2. Jot down a couple of Action Steps you can take to strengthen them.
3. Enter a reward you'll give yourself when you strengthen them.
4. Read the list each day and remind yourself to practice them.
5. Review your progress at the end of each day.

As you do this exercise, you'll be working on the causes that produce the effects of increased activities and sales.

Have you put your support/study group together yet? Please do it this week, if you haven't already. When this group continues to operate in a positive manner, with each member sharing his or her weekly application of the actions I give you, energy begins to form that you'll find very empowering for you.

Congratulations, and thank you for the privilege of joining you in your trek for greater success and increased quality of life.

3

GUIDANCE

THE CLIENT-FOCUSED SALES SYSTEM

*The only ones among you who will be really happy are
those who have sought and found a way to serve.*

—ALBERT SCHWEITZER

You'll soon know how to best serve your customers.

The next seven chapters will help you carry out your purpose statement of creating the most value for the most people. It's one thing to know you *should* be doing client-focused selling; it's another to know *how* to do it.

In this chapter you'll learn the six-step CLIENT-Focused Sales System, along with actions to take to practice each of the steps. It's important that you understand all six of these steps and their interconnection before we focus on them one at a time. My purpose is to help you do the following:

- Understand each of the steps and their purposes.
- See how each step creates a foundation for the next one.
- Know when you've completed each step.
- Know how to transition to the next step.

Then, in Chapters 4–9 you'll work on each step for a week—applying them to your real-world selling as opportunities arise. You'll develop the habit of applying the steps and also learn to use the system as a self-coaching process.

But first, let's get a complete picture of the CLIENT-Focused Sales System, and then we'll focus on one step each week in Chapters 4–9.

The CLIENT-Focused Sales System

The six steps, following the CLIENT acronym, are as follows:

1. CONNECT: Gaining comfort, trust, and rapport with clients.
2. LISTEN: Diagnosing clients' wants, needs, or desired solutions.
3. ILLUSTRATE: Explaining how you can help clients enjoy their desired benefits.
4. EVALUATE: Making sure your solutions are right for clients.
5. NEGOTIATE: Working out problems that keep clients from buying.
6. TRANSACT: Exchanging your solutions for clients' payment.

Rules for Using the System

There are four rules for using the system—making it a complete, highly effective process:

1. Decide at what point in the system you are with each person and begin at that step.

2. Complete each step before going to the next one.
3. Don't skip steps.
4. When you don't get a positive purchase decision, recognize that it's because of failure to complete one or more of the previous steps.

This is a complete system—one that can be learned on many levels and can be applied to anything you sell. With practice, you'll continue to become more effective in applying it.

Chasing Perfection

The legendary Green Bay Packers coach Vince Lombardi made this point to his team:

> Gentlemen, we will chase perfection, and we will chase it relentlessly, knowing all the while we can never attain it. But along the way, we shall catch excellence.

They never did reach perfection, but they did achieve excellence. Their plays and schemes were simple. They never tried to hide what they were going to do, but they were so well trained and conditioned that their opponents couldn't stop them—even though they could anticipate their plays.

Their desire to win, their constant practice, and their attention to detail yielded excellence on the field. This same dedication will help you catch excellence when you diligently follow the system and monitor your effectiveness.

I designed this sales system, yet I've never achieved perfection in the application of it. It's always challenging.

Before we get into the system, allow me to share with you some foundational learning principles.

Phases of Learning

If you really want to develop strong skills in applying the six-step system, follow these phases of learning:

1. Intellectually learn and understand the system.
2. Apply it in your contacts with customers.
3. Evaluate your application immediately after contacts. Go to authenticsalesperson.com, click on Tools, enter the password *authbook*, and print or download the form After Contact Self-Coaching Evaluation. This form provides a checklist that reveals to you the steps you did or didn't complete.
4. Identify what steps you implemented well and what may need improvement.

The great thinker Abraham Maslow explained the following learning phases that we go through:

1. Unconscious incompetence.
2. Conscious incompetence.
3. Conscious competence.
4. Unconscious competence.

Translated, this means:

1. We don't know what we don't know.
2. We're aware of what we don't know.

3. We're consciously learning what to do.
4. We're unconsciously doing what we've learned to do.

When you follow my directions in the next six chapters, you'll complete the first two of Maslow's four phases. Then, with conscious practice, application, and feedback, you'll ultimately perform the steps unconsciously.

So your objective is to eventually get to the point of unconscious competence.

A Paradox of Practicing the System

Practicing the six-step system is internally rewarding. It's congruent with the spirit of truth deep within your *I Am*. As you sincerely practice the CLIENT-Focused Sales System, you'll provide emotional and spiritual nourishment for the deep self-beliefs in your *I Am*. Increasing your sales. Expanding your area-of-the-possible. Releasing a higher achievement drive. Reducing call reluctance. Lowering fear of future success.

When we begin to transition from survival-, product-, or transaction-focused selling to client-focused selling, a transformation takes place inside us. Our view of selling, our view of our abilities, and our role satisfaction all change. So do our clients' views of us. Higher respect, trust, and satisfaction occur.

As you began to CONNECT with people and truly LISTEN to understand their wants or needs, your sales will dramatically increase from your previous levels. But an unexpected inner transformation will began to occur—you'll feel better about who you are and what you do. Your clients will trust you more. They gave you the respect and value that you're now demonstrating to them. Your own self-respect and deep sense of worthiness will expand.

By practicing the CLIENT-Focused Sales System, you'll have a guide to follow that will give you confidence in contacting and interacting with people.

The CLIENT-Focused Sales System Incorporates Values and Spiritual Laws

The system gives you a step-by-step road map for applying basic, paradoxical spiritual laws. As you've learned, when you choose to practice these laws, you'll trigger strong, positive emotions that will energize you and help you perform the necessary activities that create more and better value for your clients or customers. The result is increased sales and quality of life.

Here are some values, or spiritual laws, that I've woven through this book:

- I do the right thing because it's the right thing to do.
- I go the extra mile and give customers more than they expect of me.
- I focus on understanding and filling the needs of people, believing that when I do, my own needs will be met.
- I tell the truth in all situations, unless it would hurt someone.
- I do unto others as I would want them to do unto me.
- I know I'll enjoy high levels of prosperity when I create high value for others.

When you believe in and apply these values, or spiritual laws, you'll experience significant increases in your business. Granted, these values often are counter to our own self-focused, ego-driven motivations. They certainly are in opposition to much of the sales training taught in the past—closing techniques, overcoming stalls and objections, and negotiation ploys.

The good news is that when sincerely applied, they work—helping you enjoy greater self-respect, loyalty, and respect from customers.

The following pages will show you the six-step CLIENT-Focused Sales System and specific Actions to practice. Then, in Chapters 4–9, you'll focus and dig deeper, spending a week learning about and practicing each one in your daily selling activities. I call it *experiential learning*—learning by experience.

You'll notice that each of the six steps has four actions to practice, or ways to carry out each step.

Please absorb each step and its accompanying Actions to get a complete understanding of the system and its application.

The CLIENT-Focused Sales System

Step 1. CONNECT: Gaining Comfort, Trust, and Rapport with Clients

Actions

1. Focus on your purpose of creating value for people.
2. Ask questions about them and their interests.
3. Do 80 percent of the listening and 20 percent of the talking.
4. Mirror your clients' emotional tone.

Checklist to See If You've Completed the CONNECT Step

☐ People seem comfortable and open to you.
☐ They seem ready to move on and share their needs or wants with you.

☐ They indicate that they are willing to continue to your diagnostic LISTEN Step.

☐ You can get all the people together who will have input into your information gathering.

How to Transition to Your LISTEN Step—Explain that you need to understand more about their wants or needs before you can determine whether you have the best solution. Find out if this is a good time to proceed, or if you should wait until other decision makers are involved.

Step 2. LISTEN: Diagnosing Clients' Wants, Needs, or Desired Solutions

Actions

1. Ask questions about your client's current and desired situations to see if they discover and admit gaps.
2. Ask them if they are satisfied with those gaps.
3. Ask them what rewards they'd enjoy if those gaps are filled.
4. Ask them what the consequences of not closing the gaps might be.

Checklist to See If You've Completed the LISTEN Step

☐ Clients have admitted to experiencing a gap between where they now are and where they'd like to be—their current and desired situations.

☐ They've talked about the rewards they'd enjoy if the gaps were closed.

☐ They've admitted what the consequences might be if they
don't close the gaps.

☐ They've admitted a desire for a solution and are willing to
talk to you about one.

How to Transition to Your ILLUSTRATE Step—If they're open
to your solutions, paraphrase your understanding of their objectives,
and move to your ILLUSTRATE Step if all the decision makers are
present.

Step 3. ILLUSTRATE: Explaining How You Can Help Clients Enjoy Their Desired Benefits

Actions

1. Refer back to the client's admitted wants or needs.
2. Explain the features and benefits that will satisfy their
wants or needs.
3. Ask for feedback throughout your presentation.
4. Present the price at the right time.

Checklist to See If You've Completed the ILLUSTRATE Step

☐ Clients understand your recommendation and believe it
will fill their wants or needs.

☐ Their questions and concerns have been successfully answered.

☐ Everyone who has decision influence has been included in
your presentation.

☐ You've identified any roadblocks or concerns they have
about making a decision.

How to Transition to Your EVALUATE Step—Before going further, explain that you want to make sure your solution is right for them and that it will give them the benefits they desire. Ask for permission to review the highlights of your offering. Then move to the EVALUATE Step.

Step 4. EVALUATE: Making Sure Your Solutions Are Right for Clients

Actions

1. Review clients' desired benefits.
2. Show how they will enjoy extra value above the cost.
3. Find out what concerns remain unanswered.
4. Address concerns.

Checklist to See If You've Completed the EVALUATE Step

- ☐ You've reviewed what the client wants to achieve and the benefits they want to enjoy.
- ☐ You've secured agreement again that this is what they want to achieve.
- ☐ You've responded to any further questions or concerns.
- ☐ They have agreed that the value you can give them is worth more than the cost.

How to Transition to Your NEGOTIATE Step—You might ask, "Is there anything else we need to discuss before we finalize this transaction?" If the answer is yes, then go to the NEGOTIATE Step. If it is no, proceed to the TRANSACT Step.

Step 5. NEGOTIATE: Working Out Problems That Keep Clients from Buying

Actions

1. Ask where they are in their decision process.
2. Listen to and paraphrase your understanding.
3. Identify specific concerns and get agreement that they want to solve them.
4. Ask for their opinions for best solutions and seek a win-win resolution.

Checklist to See If You've Completed the NEGOTIATE Step

☐ You understand the client's concerns, if any.

☐ They believe you sincerely want to help them.

☐ You've worked through their concerns.

☐ They have no more concerns or questions.

How to Transition to Your TRANSACT Step—Make sure you've dealt with all their concerns and they're ready to buy. Go to your TRANSACT Step to find out what actions or details they want to pursue to finalize the sale.

Step 6. TRANSACT: Exchanging Your Solutions for Clients' Payment

Actions

1. Ask what details you need to discuss at this point.
2. Listen and address each issue.
3. Review how the value exceeds the cost.
4. Ask to complete the transaction.

Checklist to See If You've Completed the TRANSACT Step

☐ Everyone's concerns have been successfully worked through.

☐ The client understands how the benefits of your products or service will exceed the cost.

☐ They want what you have.

☐ They're ready to take the appropriate purchase action.

Developing Conscious Competence

Let me remind you to transfer these steps onto cards or enter them in your electronic device so you can refer to them often. Beginning with Chapter 4, focus on one of the steps each week for the next six weeks. Apply the steps in every situation that calls for them. After doing this, evaluate your success.

In time, this focused practice will help you develop an unconscious competence through which you'll automatically apply the steps at the appropriate moments.

Understanding Different Personality Patterns

All people exhibit different behavior types or Personality Patterns. Each pattern has strengths and weaknesses in performing the CLIENT-Focused Sales System. Each client will not come to a decision in the same way, want information presented the same way, want the same kind of client-seller relationship, or want to buy at the same speed. For you to communicate effectively with clients of different Personality

Patterns you must be able to shift gears and adjust to their pace, tones, and attitudes.

Consider the following model:

PERSONALITY PATTERNS MODEL

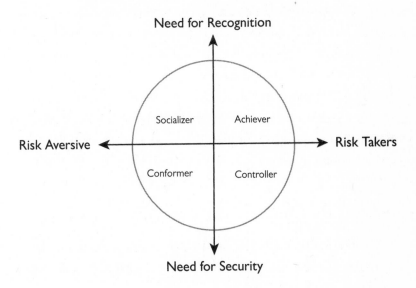

Socializers are outgoing, friendly, and affable. They like people and are vibrant and fun to be with. They're easy to approach and talk to. They buy from people they like. They often find making decisions difficult because they don't like to reject or disappoint people—even salespeople. They need social approval, recognition, and acceptance, and their greatest fear is loss of social approval.

Achievers are bottom-line, get-it-done people. They're pressed for time, action-oriented, decisive types who want to deal with the top person. They make quick decisions once they think they have a grasp of the facts. They crave respect for their achievements. Their greatest fear is loss of power.

Conformers are easygoing, steady, dependable, and loyal. They want to proceed slowly and gather as much information as possible. They're detail-minded and don't make quick decisions. They usually prefer to work in the background rather than take center stage. They're team players. They need predictability and security. Their greatest fear is taking risks.

Controllers are reserved and distant. They're logical and unemotional. They want facts and accurate information and aren't swayed by enthusiasm and personality—they may even be turned off by it. They're very analytical and well organized, and they make decisions only after carefully digesting all the facts and data. Their greatest fear is being wrong.

Important Points to Understand About Personality Patterns

As you review the model and the description of each pattern, please remember the following important points. They'll help you understand the model more easily.

1. No pattern should be considered better than another.
2. People exhibiting certain patterns tend to fit particular jobs more easily.
3. People are generally combinations of two patterns, with one being dominant, the other secondary.
4. Usually the combinations are of contiguous patterns. For example, a person could be a Socializer/Achiever or an Achiever/Socializer, an Achiever/Controller or a Controller/Achiever, and so on.

5. More complex people are often combinations of three patterns, with the third one consciously developed.

6. It takes a combination of all patterns to make a good team.

7. Salespeople tend to sell and communicate consistently with their own natural pattern; consequently, they often unwittingly misunderstand and fail to communicate with people of other patterns.

8. Rapport is achieved faster when you alter your pattern to match other people's patterns.

9. With practice, you can identify and match others' patterns unconsciously.

10. Each pattern wants information presented in unique ways, and people naturally make decisions differently.

11. Your customers' motivations are largely colored by their Personality Patterns.

Identify Your Own Patterns

On page 88, you'll find a Personality Patterns Assessment. You can use it to determine your own patterns as well as your clients'. For continual use, you can go to the Diagnostics section at the end of this book and follow the instructions for downloading the forms.

To learn the most from the process, first, for the person you are analyzing, check off each of the four descriptors that best match the traits listed on the left-hand side of the page. Then total them at the bottom of the page and see which patterns they match. Chances are you'll see a combination of two different patterns, with one being dominant and the other secondary. Occasionally, a few people are combinations of three patterns. This is rare.

Use the forms before and after contact with people, analyzing how your patterns might clash or connect with theirs. When you assess other people's patterns, think how you might blend your pattern to connect with theirs.

How to Benefit the Most from This Chapter

This week you'll spend time understanding the CLIENT-Focused Sales System and the Personality Patterns Assessment. To gain the most from this chapter, please do these activities:

1. If you haven't already done so, transfer the six-step system to cards or your electronic device. You'll need to have it handy from now on so you can use it as a guide.

2. Apply as many of the six steps as you can with each of your client contacts this week. Don't worry about your degree of effectiveness this week, as you'll work more on these steps in the chapters to come.

3. After each contact ask yourself these questions:
   a. Which of the six steps did I consciously apply?
   b. Which did I unconsciously apply?
   c. How is this different from the way I've been selling?
   d. How might I benefit from practicing the CLIENT-Focused Sales System?

4. Download the Personality Patterns Assessment by following the instructions in the Diagnostics section at the end of this book and fill one in before and after each of your client contacts this week. As you fill these in and make contact with clients, ask yourself the following:
   a. What similarities do we seem to have?
   b. What differences might we have?

    c. What might I need to do to communicate more effectively with this person?

    d. How would this person like information presented to him or her?

    e. How would this person like to make decisions?

    f. How might I be miscommunicating with this person?

    You'll learn much more about Personality Patterns in the chapters to come.

5. Meet with your study group.

    a. Share your understanding of the six-step system and the Personality Patterns process.

    b. Discuss what each of you is learning so far in your meetings.

    c. Share how you've practiced the processes this past week.

The overall purpose of this week's activities is to intellectually learn the CLIENT-Focused Sales System and the language of Personality Patterns. In the weeks to come, you'll begin to develop habits of applying both of these processes—and increase your effectiveness as time goes by.

PERSONALITY PATTERNS ASSESSMENT

1. Nature:	☐	Outgoing	☐	Dominating	☐	Easygoing	☐	No-Nonsense
2. Pace:	☐	Energetic	☐	Fast	☐	Steady	☐	Controlled
3. Manner:	☐	Friendly	☐	Dominating	☐	Accepting	☐	Evaluating
4. Conversation:	☐	People	☐	Bottom Line	☐	Systems	☐	Facts
5. Responsiveness:	☐	Friendly/Affable	☐	Impatient/Restless	☐	Steady/Resolved	☐	Cool/Distant
6. Decisions:	☐	Popular/Emotional	☐	Quick/Impulsive	☐	Slow/Studied	☐	Objective/Fact-Based
7. Time Usage:	☐	Socializes at Expense of Time	☐	Always Pushed for Time	☐	Respects Time but Not Pushed	☐	Values and Manages Time Well
8. Listening:	☐	Drifting	☐	Impatient	☐	Willing	☐	Selective
9. Talks About:	☐	People	☐	Bottom-Line	☐	Functions	☐	Organization
10. Wants Money to:	☐	Spend	☐	Gratify Ego	☐	Save	☐	Invest
11. Gestures:	☐	Open	☐	Animated	☐	Measured	☐	Closed
12. Personal Needs:	☐	Social Outlets	☐	Opportunity	☐	Security	☐	Control
13. Appearance:	☐	Scattered	☐	Flamboyant	☐	Conservative	☐	Traditional
14. Speech:	☐	Animated/Colorful	☐	Direct/Authoritative	☐	Low Keyed/Yielding	☐	Logical/Unemotional
15. Social Skills:	☐	Empathizes	☐	Commands	☐	Accepts	☐	Assesses
16. Rewarded by:	☐	Enjoyment	☐	Prestige	☐	Peace-of-Mind	☐	Secure Increases
17. Often Described as:	☐	Fun-Loving	☐	Aggressive	☐	Agreeable	☐	Critical
18. Relationship Based on:	☐	Personality	☐	Performance	☐	Common Interests	☐	Trust
19. Fears:	☐	Loss of Social Approval	☐	Loss of Successful Identity	☐	Loss of Personal Security	☐	Loss of Control
20. Motivated by:	☐	Pleasure and Relationships	☐	Pride of Ownership	☐	Peace of Mind	☐	Order and Security
		Socializer		Achiever		Conformer		Controller

Your pattern is:

Dominant_____ Secondary_____

PART II

PRACTICING THE SIX-STEP CLIENT-FOCUSED SALES SYSTEM

The more one forgets himself—by giving himself to a cause to serve or another person to love—the more human he is and the more he actualizes himself.

—VIKTOR FRANKL, *MAN'S SEARCH FOR MEANING*

4

CONNECT

GAINING COMFORT, TRUST, AND
RAPPORT WITH CLIENTS

Good listeners generally make more sales than good talkers.

—B. C. HOLWICK

Few people know how to make the first sale—to connect.

Adam Goff learned that a significant amount of selling takes place during the CONNECT Step, although there appears to be no selling happening at all.

In calling on the HR director of a hospital he'd been unable to sell to before, the moment he sat down in her office she impatiently said, "All right, show me what you've got." So, responding to her request, he pulled out brochures and began to tell her how his company's benefit policies worked. After about ten minutes, he noticed that she looked very confused and bored and seemed uninterested in what he was saying.

Thinking back to the six-step system he'd learned in our course, it dawned on him that he hadn't gained rapport with her and had allowed her impatience to cause him to jump to a product presentation much too quickly. So he put his materials aside and asked her if they could just get to know each other a bit. She nodded, and he asked her some questions, one of which was about her family. In the course of the conversation, she mentioned that her husband was disabled because of an accident a few years earlier.

Adam asked her if her husband had been able to keep his benefits from his previous employer, and she told him that he had not. She paused for a moment, then asked him to close the door to her office. She then spent more than an hour telling him how hurt her family was because the company her husband was with for so many years would not allow them to keep the benefits they had.

Adam just listened to her, and he could feel her pain. Nothing else was discussed about what he was selling, but after a while, the director quickly switched her conversation and told him that she would talk to her CEO about changing all the hospital's benefits to his company.

The next day she called him and told him that they were going to give him all their business. She went on, "Adam, I want you to know that we aren't doing this just for the benefits, we're doing it because we want you to be our agent."

The next week he wrote $55,000 in annual premiums, and later he wrote an additional $100,000. Adam now conducts monthly new-employee orientation sessions for them, and they look at him as a partner of the hospital, not just a vendor.

Let's stop for a moment and analyze the sale he made. It certainly wasn't a typical sales presentation, was it? But it was a sale. Right? So what caused it to be made?

Selling Begins During the CONNECT Step

According to my friend Price Pritchett, PhD, in the first twentieth of a second that we come into contact with another person, before we say a word we send unconscious signals to that person. In that short period of time, they tend to automatically mimic, mirror, or loop back to us what they involuntarily, unconsciously picked up from our communication. He goes on, "Words count for nothing. We literally have one twentieth of a second to shape or influence their automatic responses to us. We are literally wired to get inside the minds of others. Our demeanor gets read by others in this split second, and they mirror it back to us without conscious thought."

This is amazing, isn't it?

The CONNECT Step is the first "sale" you should focus on making. Whether it's the first time or the fifty-first time you contact customers, focus first on connecting with them. Getting them talking, and you listening. Asking questions. Listening. Valuing them. Understanding them. Gaining rapport. Being comfortable with each other.

You've completed this "first sale" when a client says with their words, body language, eye contact, and demeanor, "I've just cut out the rest of the world and am ready to listen to you."

The following four actions will help you do this.

CLIENT-Focused Sales System

Step 1. CONNECT: Gaining Comfort, Trust, and Rapport with Clients

CONNECT Actions to Practice

1. Focus on your purpose of creating value for clients.
2. Ask questions about the client and their interests.
3. Do 80 percent of the listening and 20 percent of the talking.
4. Mirror their emotional tone.

We'll think about each of these four actions, how you can apply them, and the benefits of each.

ACTION 1. FOCUS ON YOUR PURPOSE OF CREATING VALUE FOR CLIENTS

One of the largest sales I ever made was to the Shaklee Corporation. One of their field leaders had gotten me an appointment with Jack Wilder, their vice president of sales. I'd researched their field's needs thoroughly, visited with a number of their field leaders, and felt like I could help them increase the sales of their new product line, which, after an initial blitz, wasn't going well.

I went to San Francisco on a Sunday afternoon for a Monday morning meeting and stayed at a hotel just around the corner from their office, then at 444 Market Street. The evening before, to prepare my mind, I walked over to the opposite side of the street from their office, stood on the sidewalk, and stared at the building. I began to tell myself, "As big as this company is, I know ways to help them that they don't know."

I knew that because of their product line slowdown, their employee recruiting wasn't going well either. Standing there looking up at this high-rise building, I continued to talk to myself. I repeated these statements to myself:

- "I don't need to make this sale unless I can help them sell more."
- "I can do more for them than they can do for me."
- "If I'm right for them, they'll want me to help them."
- "If I do for them what I believe I can, I should earn a lot of money."

The rest of the evening I thought of all the ways I could help them. This exercise prepared my mind to confidently make the call the next day, which ultimately resulted in a sale.

After a number of visits and discussions with Jack Wilder and field people, I wrote a nine-week Slim Up & Live Course for them. Around 8,000 of their independent distributors were trained to conduct it, and thousands of people completed the course. Product sales rose. I was well compensated with new friends, money, and experience from the project. The company and distributors earned many times what I did—which I considered a big win for both of us.

My continuing *purpose* was to create as much value for them as I could, knowing that I'd be compensated consistently. So I stayed in touch with their field and home office people for the next year or so. Many people's lives were touched. It was a great experience.

Your Purpose Triggers Consistent Actions

Your real purpose will automatically trigger consistent actions— when the cause is right, the effects will be right. A genuine client-focused purpose drives behaviors that aim to create value. Other focuses—transaction, product, or survival—coming more from a self focus rather than a client focus, tend to communicate that it's about you winning instead of them benefiting.

Communication happens both on conscious and unconscious levels. Some experts believe that up to 90 percent of communication happens on subliminal levels between people. The client can make conscious judgments from your dress, mannerisms, and demeanor. Additionally, their unconscious emotional and spiritual receptors pick up your intent in nonverbal language through intuition. In our language, our *I Am* instantly communicates with other people's *I Am* dimensions—*Soul* to *Soul*. Spirit of truth to spirit of truth.

Emerson wrote, "Who you are speaks so loudly that I can't hear what you say."

Your real intent, purpose, or reason for what you do will influence not only your actions and behavior, but also your expectations. All this is being broadcast, and received by clients, through unconscious channels. While we understand so little about this phenomenon now, I believe the near future will open up much deeper understandings of it.

Here are a few of the ways we send signals that are communicated to people both consciously and subliminally:

- Moods
- Body language
- Fears
- Values
- Level of positivity or negativity
- Level of self-value
- Confidence
- Sincerity
- Comfort level

Your Actions Will Carry Out Your Real Purpose

Drill your purpose statement into your mind by constant self-suggestion. Say it to the person in the mirror. Make it your elevator statement. When people ask you what you do, repeat it to them. Don't tell them what you sell; tell them the benefits you help your clients enjoy. Buy into it intellectually, emotionally, and spiritually.

Focus your mind on doing business this way. When your purpose is genuinely to create the most value for clients, you'll perform the right actions to meet this goal. The actions you're learning will be much easier to carry out when you value a client focus. When you sincerely believe it's the best way for you to do business. When you believe it's the best way to serve your clients as well as earn a high income. When it becomes who you are.

As I suggested in Chapter 1, your intent will create the fact. You'll automatically convert your purpose into your actions.

ACTION 2. ASK QUESTIONS ABOUT THE CLIENT AND THEIR INTERESTS

An early mentor of mine once taught me a valuable lesson. J. Henry Thompson represented Diebold, Inc., one of the lines we carried when I was just out of college selling office equipment. One day while making calls with me, he observed me immediately trying to get a purchasing agent to buy a system from me that I thought he needed. No warm-up. No chitchat. No questions were asked of the client. No attempt at rapport. No nothin'!

I didn't know any better. I thought that selling was telling people what I sold and asking if they'd like to buy it.

Mr. Thompson must have suddenly developed a gigantic case of acid indigestion as he watched and listened to me rave on about this great ledger tray that I thought this company needed. He was a very dignified, elegant, and professional man and did nothing to try to "save" me . . . until we were in my car.

As I was about to drive away, he said some words to me that I've never forgotten. Very casually, he said, "You know, Ron, when you call on people, instead of doing all the talking, you may want to ask them questions and get them talking. People like to talk about themselves, and when you ask questions about them and their interests, and then listen, you'll connect better with them."

I have never forgotten that lesson.

Mr. Thompson taught me a question that day that has been of inestimable help to me when connecting with clients. The question is, "What are some things that helped get you where you are today?"

This is a question that everyone wants to answer. Mr. Thompson explained different ways I could ask the question. "How did you get into accounting?" "What are some of the main things that have helped you become so successful?" "What advice would you have for someone who wanted to be successful like you?"

This gave me much more self-confidence when approaching people. In time I learned that much of my fear of rejection stemmed from worrying that I couldn't communicate well with older purchasing agents or other managers. After that, instead of trying to impress people or control the conversation, all I had to do was ask questions and get people talking. This in itself completely changed my view of selling. But what it mainly did was help me gain quicker and stronger rapport with people.

This was one of the most important lessons I learned about selling. My fears of being able to communicate with customers virtually went away.

I found that when I asked clients these questions—and sincerely wanted to know their answers—amazing things happened. Connections occurred that wouldn't have otherwise happened. Clients would answer my questions, seeming to assume that I thought and understood things on the same level they did. I didn't have to "sell" myself; as they answered my questions, they "bought" me.

I sincerely wish Mr. Thompson were still alive today, as I'd love to thank him for sharing that question with me, tell him ways I've applied it, and show how I've shared it with thousands of course participants and readers of my books.

Structure Questions According to the Level of the Relationship

Regardless of your relationship with clients, or how often you contact or call on them, you can plan to ask appropriate questions that draw them out and get them talking.

Obviously, you'll ask different questions of different people. If it's your first contact with them, your questions will be focused on learning more about them—either personal or business. "How did you get into this business?" "Do you live in this neighborhood?" "What do you do for a living?" "How long have you been at your current job?"

Or it may be that you have frequent contact with your customers and have gotten to know them on a deeper level. Questions like these may be appropriate: "How was your vacation?" "What university is your son going to?" "How are you and your family enjoying your new home?"

Fit the question to the situation, relationship, appropriateness, or Personality Patterns of the people with whom you're communicating:

- *Socializers* want to talk about friendships, other people, outside-of-work activities, family, fun things they do, groups they are involved in, hobbies they have.
- *Achievers* want to talk about themselves, their accomplishments, results, how they run things, powerful people they know, how they became successful.
- *Conformers* want to talk about stability, tried-and-true methods, how they maintain things and keep them in good working order, their job activities and details, product and people loyalty, how to get the most value in purchases.
- *Controllers* want to talk about order, organization, attention to details, efficiency, logical issues, problem solving, what could go wrong with things, how to keep problems from happening.

You'll naturally want to talk about things that are driven by your own Personality Patterns, but then you run the risk of miscommunication with people who have different patterns than you. Determining other people's patterns is another reason for asking questions and listening to the answers. Listening to and observing their choice of words, pace, tone, body language, and environment can give you clues as to what subjects interest your customer.

Of course, you won't always be totally accurate, but just listening to them and trying to understand them will get you ahead of most other salespeople. In time, you'll begin to unconsciously mirror your client's pace, tone, and attitudes.

While we'll never get perfect at matching others people's patterns, it's the constant trying to understand them, and adapting to them, that causes us to get better and better at doing it.

ACTION 3. DO 80 PERCENT OF THE LISTENING AND 20 PERCENT OF THE TALKING

The great author Rudyard Kipling, when asked the key to his excellent writing skills, wrote this:

> I keep six honest serving men (They taught me all I knew);
> Their names are What and Why and When and How and Where
> and Who.

These key words get customers doing 80 percent of the talking. We spend our 20 percent asking questions with one of these six "honest serving men" and responding with more questions about them. We spend the other 80 percent listening to the client's responses and understanding them.

Before I learned this action, I couldn't connect with Mr. Ketler. He was the manager of a savings and loan company that was associated with about ten building, insurance, title, and other companies. I'd called on him several times, and each time, before I could get close to his office, he'd look up through the glass that encased his cubicle, and yell out, "We don't want anything."

As this little exchange happened, I'd turn sixteen shades of crimson and look for the nearest hole to crawl into. He was a small man with the bark of a timber wolf. You could hear him for blocks. It was embarrassing beyond words. All the workers would look up from their desks at me. They were all probably placing bets: "How long will this young kid keep coming by here, and how will he rank with the other salespeople that Mr. Ketler has run off?"

They may even have had an office pool where they drew numbers that had specific days that I'd quit calling on him.

This client was an Achiever/Controller off the charts.

After reflecting on Mr. Thompson's advice about asking questions and listening, I called Mr. Ketler and told him who I was, and he quickly replied, "We don't want anything."

I replied, "I'm not trying to sell you anything."

"Then what do you want?" he asked.

"I'd like to get some advice from you," I replied.

"About what?"

"About some property that's for sale."

He invited me to come by. He spent an hour giving me his opinion about the property. At the end of this time he asked, "You got time for a cup of coffee?" Well, being a salesperson, I had plenty of time for coffee.

He began to buy from me. He even began to call me at home in the evenings and ask me to come by the next day. He must have worked thirty-two hours a day. We developed a great relationship.

He was a very intelligent man, and I respected him a lot. As with most people exhibiting his Personality Patterns, when you've passed their tests of trust, and connected with them, they'll be very loyal, taking a sincere interest in you and wanting to help you out.

Soon, all his other companies were buying their furniture, systems, equipment, and supplies from me. Because I listened to him, I established a rapport that lasted until I opened my own interior design and retail furniture business five years later.

Ways to Enhance Your First Impression

You can enhance the first impression you make by following these simple communication suggestions.

- Allow clients to finish all their thoughts, sentences, and paragraphs—don't interrupt.
- Resist the urge to go off on tangents about yourself, your ideas, or your experiences.
- Ask clarifying questions in response to what clients say.
- Seek to understand what they're saying, how they feel, and what's important to them.
- Neither agree nor disagree—just listen and understand.
- Resist offering your opinions unless they're asked for.

Observe how other people listen to you or others, and you'll see that few of them demonstrate good listening skills. How many people do you know who never allow you to finish a sentence and don't even realize that they constantly interrupt?

How to Prove You're Hearing and Understanding

Giving feedback while you're listening proves you're hearing and understanding. Here are some ways to give feedback.

- Keep eye contact.
- Nod approval when clients say something you believe to be correct.
- Verbalize reinforcement by saying, "I understand," or "Thank you for saying that."
- Ask for further explanations. "Please tell me more." "Explain to me how you did that." "What else did you learn?"
- When things clients say remind you of your own experiences, and you are tempted to jump in and tell your story . . . don't.

Practicing these simple listening skills will help you connect with people, and you'll achieve a level of rapport that others fail to attain.

ACTION 4. MIRROR THEIR EMOTIONAL TONE

Every one of us has our own emotional and physical cadence—the energy patterns, rhythm, or tempo to which we march.

- *Socializers* have an up-and-down cadence, depending on whether they're talking or listening. They're usually not good listeners and can get bored, disinterested, and distracted when they are not the center of attention. You'll get plenty of talk from them. They get excited when talking about other people and things they enjoy doing.

- *Achievers* often have high energy and are usually involved in result-producing activities. Things need to move fast for them. They can run roughshod over people of other patterns, unless others match their energy levels. If you're another pattern, watch for signs that they want you to move faster and focus less on the details. They like to do business with other strong people.

- *Conformers* have a slow, steady, unhurried pace. Typically risk-averse, they want to go slow and get things done right. They're usually distance runners and not sprinters. Achievers can overpower them. In the pure form, Socializers may not be serious enough for them.

- *Controllers* usually have a low emotional tone, will logically assess you, and will often give you yes or no answers, rather than a long explanation. You'll get little feedback from them and may not be sure what they're actually thinking.

To mirror people's emotional tones, you can adopt their physical energy and positioning, speak with similar volume, and match their verbal pace and tempo.

Whatever you do to match their patterns, your intent must be to sincerely understand them and not to manipulate them. If your actions aren't sincere, most people will get the message pretty quickly.

Allow People to Help You

I was at first very nervous about calling on older, more successful people when I began to sell office equipment. I was twenty-one, and most of the purchasing agents I called on were two to three times my age. In time, Mr. Thompson's advice and Mr. Ketler's relationship taught me a principle that helped me a lot. I learned that successful people will gladly share their knowledge and help younger people who sincerely want to learn.

When I began practicing this wise principle, I found that I could get in to see more successful people than before. I prefaced my initial contact with this statement: "I'm a young salesman who wants to be successful like you. Would you mind sharing with me some ideas that helped you get where you are today?" Clients are honored by this question. The more successful they are, the more they want to answer this question.

I was always welcome when my visits were to report on how their advice was working for me. I rarely asked them to buy from me, because when I developed relationships with them, they wanted to buy from me.

Along this line, I recently received an email from one of our graduates, John Bizal, new to the financial services business, who called on a prominent member of his community, only to be bluntly told up front, "Everyone knows someone like you who has entered the financial services industry for six months, couldn't make it, and then moved on."

The executive's message was clear: "Why do you think I'd allow someone as inexperienced as you to help me and my company with our financial situations?"

"You can only imagine how deflated I was after this comment," John said in his email.

Fortunately he had the presence of mind to apply the CONNECT actions to redirect the conversation and get the executive talking about himself and his interests. "After this," he went on, "I addressed the elephant in the room. I asked him if he could refer other people to me. He opened up and began naming a few people who he thought would be of interest for me to speak with.

"Here he was moments ago telling me he'd have to see how long I made it in the business before I'd have any credibility with him. Now he was willing to refer people to me. This didn't make sense, and I respectfully told him it didn't. He agreed and gracefully acknowledged it as well.

"I left the meeting with him telling me that he'd start small with me, and see how things would go. He agreed to put me in touch with his CFO, start with a few items, and see what happens."

I emailed John back and suggested that he position himself as this man's pupil, asking to come by occasionally and learn more about how the executive had become so successful.

After this learning experience, John's monthly sales tripled from what they had been before. Who knows, this may have been the turning point that kept him in the business.

Highly successful people need to perpetuate their success by transferring their ideas into the minds of people who sincerely want to learn. When we do this, and then occasionally report back to them about how we are applying their ideas, we repay them well for the gift they gave us.

Understand What People Want to Talk About

Understanding what clients want to talk about is easy if they're Socializers—they want to talk about themselves, and their interests.

A number of years ago I did some one-day seminars for a national company. To initially sell the deal, I was asked to meet with a man named John. We met at a restaurant near O'Hare in Chicago. At first he seemed to be a bit bored with the details of having to meet me. I found out pretty quickly that he loved to talk. His Personality Pattern was obvious from the beginning of our meeting—Socializer through and through.

As we were eating, the server walked behind me, and John's eyes followed her movements; he was quite actively and analytically distracted from looking at or listening to me.

When his eyes finally came back to me, I asked him, "John, at what age did you go from being a dirty *young* man to a dirty *old* man?"

He looked at me and about died laughing. He seemed to think that was the funniest thing he'd ever heard. It was like I couldn't have complimented him more. We immediately became fast friends, and his organization became a very good client.

Would I say something like that to just anyone? Of course not. If I asked that question of Controllers, they'd dismiss me immediately, seeing no humor in it—changing the subject to the last time they read *War and Peace*. Or they'd spend the rest of the afternoon lecturing me on political correctness. Achievers would give it a quick laugh and move on to more important things, like what they want to talk about—themselves and their successes. Conformers might be offended or feel uncomfortable, or the ones with higher-than-natural confidence would suggest that I pray for forgiveness. The ones with less confidence would just pray silently for me.

Your Questions Can Help You Determine the Interests of Clients

On first contact it's good to ask questions that will help you discover what people want to talk about. Is it:

- Business
- Personal life
- Social life
- Hobbies, or personal interests
- Other

Here are some questions that have opened up a useful dialogue between me and potential customers:

- How long have you had this job or position?
- What do you most like about it?
- What kind of changes have taken place in it in the last few years?
- What changes do you anticipate happening in the next few years?
- How have these changes affected you?
- What do you do in your spare time?
- What would you do if you didn't have to work?

One of the mistakes we can make is to assume that everyone wants to talk about the same things we do. So if we're Socializers wanting to connect with Controllers, we'll likely try to be too friendly. They want sales interactions to be based on logic and facts, not on emotions.

Achievers will run over Conformers; Conformers will bore Achievers. Controllers can be skeptical of Socializers' promises; Socializers can be offended by Controllers' lack of emotional connection with them.

The Three Levels of Communication

Do you make onetime sales, where you don't have ongoing communication with your clients, or do you have continual relationships with them? In both cases, gaining rapport is crucial.

In onetime sales, it's still important to take a moment or two and connect with people, as a cashier at the airport parking lot did for me recently. When I handed her my ticket, she looked at me, smiled, and said, "Good afternoon, how has your day been going?" There was a special sincerity in her smile and greeting. She noticed me. It was like she stopped her world for a few seconds to focus on me. Which she did.

Or your customers may be people you serve on a regular basis, for whom you continue to provide benefits and create value. It's still important to take a few moments, depending on their Personality Patterns, and apply these CONNECT actions.

As we saw from Adam Goff's example at the beginning of this chapter, our initial questions can cause people to share emotional feelings and open up to us. Most often, though, they'll begin interaction with you on a more logical, safe, guarded level of communication. I remember finally selling to companies after calling on them for several months. It had taken me that length of time to gain significant rapport with them, to the point at which they'd consider buying from me.

THE THREE LEVELS OF CONSCIOUSNESS

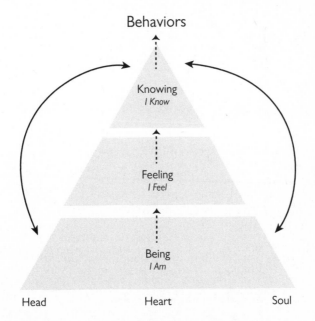

It helps to understand the Three Levels of Communication, and to adjust your questions and expectations accordingly. Consider our Three Levels of Consciousness model for a moment. Let's equate the consciousness levels with the communication levels:

1. At the *I Know* level, the communication is, "I hear you, I understand what you're saying, and I will communicate with you in a logical, realistic manner."
2. At the *I Feel* level, the communication is, "I feel good about you, I'm open to you, and we can share our feelings with relative safety."
3. At the *I Am* level, the communication is, "I trust you, we have similar values and beliefs, and we can communicate on the deepest levels of sincerity and honesty."

As we understand these communication levels and are sensitive to them, we'll have a guide to follow. This way we won't expect people to trust us without giving them the time and experience to prove that they are right to do so. Nor will we ask insensitive, personal questions when we are still on an *I Know* communication level with someone.

These suggestions go both ways—in our questions and expectations of others, and their questions and expectations of us. I have a friend, not a close friend, whom I see occasionally. Each time he asks me the most intimate questions that are none of his business. I usually laugh and deflect with some smart-aleck answer, but I still feel uncomfortable talking to him. He's so insensitive that he has no idea about his intrusions. For over twenty years he's never offered to pay for lunch. It's like it never dawns on him that restaurants would allow him to pay.

Remember, that the mix of our Personality Patterns can also influence our communication with others.

- Socializers want to be your friends; they go to emotional trust levels more quickly than other patterns.
- Achievers want to know how you can help them reach their goals; they will trust you when you show them how you can help them.
- Conformers will trust you when you have removed all the risks involved in your relationship or purchase.
- Controllers will remain in the logical mode longer than other patterns, trusting you because of your accuracy, no-nonsense presentations, and underpromising.

Don't Overanalyze People's Communication Levels When with Them

Assessing people's communication levels can distract you and block rapport and understanding when you're with them. Creating preoccupation. Keeping you from listening. Blocking your understanding.

Here's a tip: Before and after your contacts with people, analyze the communication levels you've attained with them. How do they want to communicate? How do they not want to communicate?

But when you're with them, don't analyze anything, just listen, understand, and focus on your purpose of creating the most value for them. This way you won't be distracted and can fully listen.

This same advice relates to understanding customers' Personality Patterns. When you're with them, don't analyze their patterns, but fully absorb who they are and what they're saying. Direct all your attention on them, their wants or needs, and how you might help them.

Then, when you come away from meetings or contacts with people, take a moment and analyze your interaction, and determine their patterns and communication levels.

CONNECT Self-Assessment

Please read each statement and ask yourself, "How descriptive is this statement of my actual behaviors with clients?" If it's always descriptive, circle 10; if it's never descriptive, circle 1; if it's sometimes descriptive, circle the appropriate number in between.

1. For my first sale, I always focus on gaining rapport with people.

    1   2   3   4   5   6   7   8   9   10

2. As quickly as I can, I always ask questions to get people talking and me listening.

    1   2   3   4   5   6   7   8   9   10

3. I totally connect with people and give them my complete attention.

    1   2   3   4   5   6   7   8   9   10

4. I always focus completely on listening and understanding who people are and what they're saying.

    1   2   3   4   5   6   7   8   9   10

5. I always get into sync with people and mirror their emotional tone.

    1   2   3   4   5   6   7   8   9   10

    Total: _____

What one behavior did you perform well? Which one would you like to improve?

How to Prepare for the CONNECT Step

In the Diagnostics section of this book, you'll find instructions for downloading the Pre-Call and Post-Call planning forms. You'll want to keep several copies of these forms. Before filling out the Pre-Call planning form, you'll want to follow these suggestions:

1. If it's your first contact, find out as much as you can about the business or individual.
2. Depending on the size of the sale, learn about what they sell, who their clients are, and what's the position of the person you're contacting.
3. Then after your contact, again depending on the size of the sale, fill in a Post-Call planning form.

Coaching Yourself on the CONNECT Step

You'll know when you've completed the CONNECT Step when:

1. You've established rapport with customers.
2. You've asked if you can get information about their wants or needs, and they've agreed.
3. They agree to set a time for you to proceed to your diagnostic LISTEN Step.
4. All the people who will have input into your information gathering can be available for the next meeting.

How to Benefit the Most from This Chapter

Write the four CONNECT actions on an index card or your electronic device—wherever they will be handy as a reminder to practice.

1. Spend a week reading and absorbing the message of this chapter, underlining points you want to remember and writing action ideas.
2. Focus on applying the four actions whenever you get the opportunity.
3. Resist the temptation to move into your product presentation or demonstration until you've completed the CONNECT Step.
4. Meet with your study group and share how you applied the ideas of this chapter, what happened when you did, and what you learned.
5. Coach yourself on the CONNECT Step by reviewing the four points under this heading, checking to make sure you've completed this step with each contact.

Again, your first step is to connect with people. Putting them at ease. Getting comfortable with them. Developing trust. Listening. Hearing. Understanding. Drawing them out.

How to Transition to the LISTEN Step

Now that you've established a rapport with your client, explain that you need to understand more about their wants or needs before you can determine whether you have the best solution for them.

Resist the temptation to proceed with a product presentation or demonstration at this point. The rule is: Don't present solutions until people have first admitted a desire for them and you feel your offerings will give them the benefits they want.

Most salespeople don't know or practice this, as they generally do product- or transaction-focused selling—prematurely explaining the features and benefits of their offerings and then asking customers to buy them.

When you've gained rapport and it's time to move on in the process, you might take a moment to explain what you do and transition to your diagnostic LISTEN Step. You can even repeat your purpose statement as an introduction. "I help organizations like yours [explain the benefits you help them enjoy]. I wouldn't know whether I have the best solutions for you until I understand more about your wants or needs. Do you mind if I ask you a few questions to see if I might be able to help you?"

Let them know that you're not trying to sell them anything, but just gathering information about their situation. This usually gets customers unfolding their arms and minds and more ready to objectively listen to you.

5

LISTEN

DIAGNOSING CLIENTS' WANTS, NEEDS, OR DESIRED SOLUTIONS

Prescription without diagnosis is malpractice.

—ANONYMOUS

Don't get trapped into premature product presentations.

That's what Jack Wilder at the Shaklee Corporation did to me the first time I called on him. When I went into his office, he shook my hand, we both sat down, and his first words were, "The only reason I'm seeing you is that I told Norman Pahmeier that I would. You have thirty minutes, what do you have?"

If you're not ready for an opening salvo like that, it can suck you immediately into a product presentation before you've had time to CONNECT or LISTEN to diagnose their situations. Skipping the first two steps of the CLIENT-Focused Sales System sets you up for a potential client to tell you he or she doesn't need what you have, and before you know it, you're out the door.

I thanked him for seeing me, deflected his question back to him, and asked, "I know how busy you must be, so I'll get to what I came to learn . . . how is your Slim Plan going?"

He looked at me and replied, "Just fine," leaning back in his chair and waiting for my response. It was obvious he wasn't going to give me any more information.

"Congratulations," I said. I paused a moment and asked, "How is your recruiting going?"

He didn't say a word for what seemed like an eternity; he finally pulled himself upright in his chair and said, "Okay, what have you got?"

I had a list of questions; I pulled them out of my briefcase and began asking them. My questions centered on these points:

- What had happened since the new product was introduced?
- Were they satisfied with the sales they were now getting?
- What would they like to see happening?
- What had they done to boost sales?
- How important was increasing their sales?

I wanted to understand the following information:

- Their current situation.
- Their level of satisfaction with their current situation.
- Their desired situation, if they weren't satisfied with their current situation.
- The rewards they'd enjoy if their desired situation was achieved.
- The consequences of not reaching their desired situation.

He gave me lots of information for the next two hours. I wasn't there to talk about solutions, but rather to gather information and to see if he would admit a need I could help them fill or a problem I could help them solve.

Finally, his assistant came into the office, apologizing for the interruption, holding a whole stack of phone messages, and said, "Jack, when are you going to be finished? All these people want to talk to you."

He took the slips and asked me, "When will you be back in San Francisco again?"

It happened that I was doing a seminar there two weeks after that, and we set a time to meet again. It took several meetings and dozens of phone calls before the sale was made, which is normal for one that size.

Remember Your Purpose

It's always good to remember your client-focused purpose when you perform the LISTEN Step. Make sure your goal is to gather information about the client's current and desired situations to determine:

- Do they have wants, needs, problems, or desired solutions that they want filled, satisfied, or solved?
- What is their sense of urgency?
- Are they open to talking to you about solutions?
- Who are the other people involved in their decision making?

You demonstrate your professionalism when your intent, words, and actions say: "My purpose is to get sufficient information that helps me understand your wants or needs to see if I have solutions that help you get what you want."

Contrast this with the implied purpose of many salespeople, whose actions seem to say, "I'm here to see if I can sell you something."

Which would impress you the most, if you were your client?

Applying This Chapter Will Elevate
Your Selling Success, Respect of Others,
and Sense of Worth

Learning about the LISTEN Step and applying it will completely change the way you sell if you've been doing the old traditional product-focused selling. The two strategies are poles apart, contrasting these following two statements:

- I want to understand what you want to accomplish, so I can see if my solutions are the best ones for you.
- I want to persuade you to buy my product or service so I'll earn more.

When the first one is your objective, you'll be favorably viewed, received, and respected. I know from working with thousands of salespeople all around the world that client-focused selling builds your own self-value. There's an inner reward that comes to you when you see yourself creating more and better value for clients. It's called *increased self-respect* and *greater sense of worth*.

The LISTEN Step also shows customers your desire to give them extra value beyond just the worth of the solution you sell. Napoleon Hill, writing in his classic *The Master Key to Riches*, makes this point:

Let us now observe that the admonition to render more service and better service than for which one is paid, is paradoxical because it is impossible for anyone to render such service without receiving appropriate compensation . . . The compensation may come in many forms and from many different sources, some of them strange and unexpected sources, but come it will.

Let's think more of the power of this step.

People Are More Likely to Take Action When It's Their Idea, Rather Than Yours

Think about these communication principles for a moment:

- People value what they tell you more than what you tell them.
- They respond more to information that is asked for than to information that is freely given to them.
- You connect more when people are talking, and you're listening, than when they're listening and you're talking.

The LISTEN Step brings you to a fork in the road. As it divides, one juncture leads to transaction- or product-focused selling. The other takes you to client-focused selling. Typically, most salespeople choose the first fork and begin talking about their products, services, or solutions, or whatever they want to sell.

Client-focused sales professionals know to delay discussions about their products or services until their customers have given them information about their current situation and their desired situation and have admitted an eagerness for a solution.

CLIENT-Focused Sales System

Step 2: LISTEN: Diagnosing Clients' Wants, Needs, or Desired Solutions

Clients don't buy anything unless there's a conflict between their current situation and what they'd like to be experiencing.

Again, the purpose of this step is not to discuss or offer solutions but to gather information. When you ask well-designed questions that draw clients out and get them talking, they'll often realize their own conflicts or gaps between where they are and where they'd like to be. Or they'll admit to a disharmony between what results they're now getting and what they'd like to be enjoying.

This conflict usually exists before we purchase anything. Think about a smiling attendant behind the popcorn counter in a movie, looking at you and saying, "Doesn't it smell great?" How long did it take her to make a sale to you? Did her question, or the wonderful aroma, create a conflict between your enjoying or not enjoying the treat during the movie? Did you buy?

People don't make purchase decisions unless there's sufficient reason to take action to relieve their conflict or enhance their gain. People are much more likely to take action when they discover and admit their own gaps. We intuitively know this, but how many times do we attempt to convince them they have conflicts that need resolving, and even though they know they do, they resist us, because it wasn't their idea? There's an old saying: *People convinced against their will are of the same opinion still.*

Let me now give you a process for obtaining information to see if a gap or conflict does exist within your clients' minds. First, think about the following actions to practice.

LISTEN Actions to Practice

1. Ask questions about clients' current and desired situations to see if they discover and admit gaps.
2. Ask them if they are satisfied with those gaps.
3. Ask them what rewards they'd enjoy if those gaps were filled.
4. Ask them what the consequences of not closing the gaps might be.

ACTION 1. ASK QUESTIONS ABOUT CLIENTS' CURRENT AND DESIRED SITUATIONS TO SEE IF THEY DISCOVER AND ADMIT GAPS

The following gap or conflict model will help you determine whether your customers have sufficient conflicts between where they now are and where they'd like to be, in order to be a prospect for your solutions.

Here's a model that gives you a simple process to effectively identify people's wants, needs, problems, or desired situations:

THE DIAGNOSTIC CONFLICT MODEL

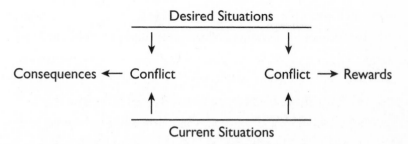

This process is a powerful way to get clients to sell themselves on your product or service, allowing you to remain in a professional counselor role. This model provides you an effective guide for gathering information and taking people through a logical analytical process. Regardless of what you're selling—from automobiles to popcorn—you can adapt specific questions that help you gather the information you need to make the sale.

The Theory of Cognitive Dissonance

Let's review Dr. Leon Festinger's concept of *cognitive dissonance*. This means having mental or emotional conflicts, or creating an inner state of disharmony. For instance, the conflict may be between who you think you are and who you think you should be, or what abilities a certain situation requires versus what abilities you feel you currently possess. Whatever creates a strong dissatisfaction between your current situation and your desired situation creates a cognitive dissonance within you and motivates you to take some kind of action.

For customers, the conflict can be between what they currently have and what they'd like to have. Generally, a state of inner conflict must exist before a customer will make a purchase decision. Wise salespeople, knowing this, never present their product or service solutions unless customers have discovered and admitted this inner conflict and a desire for some kind of resolution.

This theory can be applied during the diagnostic LISTEN Step by asking questions that get customers talking about the following:

- What they now have, and what they'd like to have.
- Where they now are, and where they'd like to be.
- What problems they now have that they'd like to solve.
- What's not happening that they'd like to be happening.

When we ask questions about their current and desired situations, and listen, people often sell themselves on needing a service.

This is especially effective when we then get them talking about the rewards of attaining their desired situation, and then the consequences of not doing so.

Sometimes you can accomplish both the CONNECT and LISTEN Steps in one meeting. Or both may take more time, depending on the size of the sale and your relationship with the buyer.

Your client's current situation can be made up of many different factors—what product or service they're currently using, from whom they're buying, their level of satisfaction with their current vendors, and so on.

Pete and Cynthia Caucci were wise enough to quickly find out that a new account they were calling on was very unhappy with their current supplier. They sell employee benefits, and one day they were asked by another advisor to service an account of his. He was sick and wanted them to keep the appointment with the owner of the company.

When they met with the owner, he asked where the other advisor was, and they told him that he was sick. He replied, "I guess he knew what was coming today, and he sent you."

They soon found out that the owner was canceling all the business the other agent had written, because of his lack of integrity and the service he'd given.

Rather than acting defensively, they apologized and began asking questions. They asked how he started his business. He told them how he grew the business from working as a meatpacker to owning nine large grocery stores. Taking plenty of time, he gladly described many of his struggles and difficulties.

Near the end of two and a half hours, Pete and Cynthia told the owner a bit about themselves, their community service, and how they did business. The owner smiled and said, "I didn't think this meeting was going to end this way." He asked them to send him a recap of the meeting. On the way out of his office he asked the payroll manager to keep all business he'd planned to cancel. The next month they wrote an additional $180,000 in premiums.

While a client's need to replace a salesperson is a bit unusual, it does show that there are many different kinds of current situations that affect the information you may need to get from your customer—depending on the complexity of the sale.

Remember, logic is not always a major part of a buyer's decisions. Emotional factors play a major role.

Your customer's current situations could include ones like these:

- What they've been buying.
- From whom they've been buying.
- Their level of satisfaction with what they've been buying.
- Changes in their business or personal lives.
- Age of what they've been buying
- How much of your product they still have on hand.
- Some internal changes in people, processes, or other requirements.

When customers tell you about their current and desired situations, and they've admitted that a gap or conflict exists between the two, you'll want to find out their urgency to achieve their desired situation. The next action will allow you to discover their state of dissatisfaction.

ACTION 2. ASK THE CLIENT IF THEY ARE SATISFIED WITH THOSE GAPS

Once you've understood your client's current situation, your next question is, "How satisfied are you with this situation as it now exists?"

If they are content, you may not have a prospect. Generally, people don't buy new things unless they are dissatisfied with the old things or situations.

If they admit a conflict between their current and desired situations, you'll want to get them talking about the size of the conflict so you can determine the degree of discomfort they're feeling. Find out what their discomfort is now costing them in money, time, efficiency, or other desired benefits. This can give you some idea of whether they'll be motivated to make a purchase decision.

Remembering that it's the *level of dissatisfaction* that usually drives a person to purchase something new, you can ask more questions to get your customers talking more about why they're dissatisfied. As they talk, they further convince themselves of their need to make a change.

ACTION 3. ASK THE CLIENT WHAT REWARDS THEY'D ENJOY IF THOSE GAPS WERE FILLED

People are often *pushed* to purchase things because of their dissatisfaction with what they've been using, but they are also *pulled* to buy things because of the rewards they'll enjoy. This push/pull effect can determine their dominant buying motives. If during the CONNECT and LISTEN Steps you discover that your customer is not satisfied with the conflicts they've admitted having, get them talking about the rewards they'll enjoy if they make a change. Once you've done this, ask what consequences they might suffer if they don't take action and close the gap.

This line of questioning allows them to sell themselves on your services. They often drop any resistance they might have shown when they first perceived you were trying to persuade them to buy from you.

You'll learn a lot of useful information when clients talk about the rewards they'll enjoy by purchasing from you. Listen carefully and you'll be able to glean their level of interest in or excitement about these new purchases. They may also express concerns or reveal deeper buying motives. Pay careful attention to determine if their desire for the rewards of purchasing from you seems to exceed their reluctance to make such a decision. Or does the pain of the problem exceed the cost of the cure?

As with your other LISTEN actions, you're asking *who, what, where, why, when,* and *how* questions to draw them out with explanations, not just to provide yes or no answers. You might ask questions like these:

- What benefits will you enjoy when you enjoy your desired situation?
- How will these directly help you?
- How will they impact your organization's bottom line?
- How will this increase your efficiency or productivity?

As they give you answers, ask for clarification, further explanation, and more details—still doing 20 percent of the talking and 80 percent of the listening.

ACTION 4. ASK THE CLIENT WHAT THE CONSEQUENCES OF NOT CLOSING THE GAPS MIGHT BE

The question here, however you phrase it, is: "What might happen if you don't move from your unacceptable current situation toward your desired situation?" In other words, you're asking them, "What will happen if you don't fix the problem you've just admitted having?" Or, "What will happen if you allow what you don't want to happen to continue happening?"

Most of us go through this thought process, regardless of what we're buying. Who of us hasn't said to ourselves, "If I don't get a haircut, I'll look shaggy for this important meeting." "If I don't lose some weight I'll be embarrassed at my college reunion." "If I don't get some new clothes, my clients will think I don't look very professional."

Take a moment and think about what your customers might consider to be negative consequences of not buying from you. Consider all kinds of motives—logical, illogical, positive, and negative. How it will affect them personally. How it will deprive them of some desired benefit. How they think it might cause them to be perceived by others.

As you think of these possible customer consequences, determine the push of the consequences versus the pull of the rewards. If the customer does not have a large enough fear of the consequences, they will often put off purchases even though their desire for the rewards is high.

Remember, people buy things for two reasons:

- Hope of gain
- Relief of pain

It's wise to determine which of these motivates your customers the most.

Be Aware of Different Personality Patterns

Whether you're talking or meeting with one person or a group of people, you'll want to be aware of their Personality Patterns. This will help you understand how to phrase your questions, their dominant buying motives, how fast they want to move, and how thorough they want your diagnostic assessment to be.

Socializers will be concerned about how people will be affected by any purchasing decision they make and how they'll personally be accepted or viewed. They'll usually want to make other people happy so that they remain well liked. Not being analytical, they may experience challenges giving you specific details when answering your questions. They'll want to know that the risks of making a decision are low.

If other people are involved in the purchasing decision, they'll probably be the dominant decision influencers—especially Controllers or Achievers. Achievers will take charge of the meeting and dominate the conversation, allowing everyone else to decide whose side to get on. Controllers often sit back without saying much, allowing the Achievers and Socializers to expound, knowing all along that they hold the keys to the money to be spent.

Achievers will be more interested in bottom-line results than the details of how those will be achieved. They can give you more information about their desired situation than the current one, as they're usually thinking ahead about how to make their future goals happen. Whereas Socializers and Conformers are usually other-people focused, Achievers tend to be more self-focused. Their concerns are more about getting credit, recognition, or acclaim for their achievements. Generally having larger egos than other patterns, Achievers will more often be interested in what will make them look good and retain their power.

Achievers aren't so much interested in reducing risks, as they are in maximizing the possible rewards.

Conformers will be more detail oriented with their questions and answers, as they're sincere, conscientious people who want to do the right things for others. If they're single buyers, you'll need to spend more time with them. They'll want to think through their answers more than other Personality Patterns. They'll be more concerned about the risks they'll run than the rewards they'll enjoy. You'll need to fully understand their perception of the specific risks they'll run if they make a purchase decision and help them reduce their fears. You might spend time understanding what Conformers' "safe zones" are—what solutions would provide them the most safety. "What solutions would help you feel most comfortable?" is a good question to ask. Another might be, "What problems or challenges would you most like to avoid?" When you allow them to verbalize their concerns and let them know you understand them, your trust and rapport is enhanced.

Ask Controllers questions about what facts, details, or specific guidelines they want to follow. Find out how they make decisions. How they want information delivered to them. They want proof of your solution efficacy. Like Conformers, they're interested in eliminating risks. But unlike Conformers, it's not the risk they're most concerned about, but the guaranteed return. They will take risks once they've clearly validated the downside.

When presenting to Controllers, play down your benefits. They will be impressed with this, but when they think you're exaggerating your claims, they'll cut you off with little emotional drain.

Just as you need to be concerned with your customers' Personality Patterns, you'll want to also think about how your own patterns will influence your LISTEN Step and how your patterns might interact with your specific clients' patterns.

Here are some ways that you might miscommunicate:

- *If you are a Socializer:* Spending too much time on matters extraneous to the subject at hand. Failing to ask enough detailed questions. Interrupting and getting off on tangents. Not listening closely to more detailed people. Talking too much. Allowing your mind to drift when you aren't talking.

- *If you are an Achiever:* Dominating the talking. Not really listening. Telling clients what you think they should have, rather than asking them what they want to have. Showing impatience with people who exhibit other patterns. Blowing through the CONNECT and LISTEN Steps and jumping too quickly to the ILLUSTRATE Step.

- *If you are a Conformer:* Yielding control to more dominant people. Asking too many process or procedure questions, rather than ones that focus on results, other concerns, or returns on investments.

- *If you are a Controller:* Showing low empathy to Socializers and Conformers, creating a discomfort within them. Socializers might think you are too serious. Achievers can think you are too nitpicky, focusing too much on the mundane.

Remember that few people are single quadrant patterns; most of us are combinations of two contiguous ones, although one will usually be dominant.

Find Out Their Sense of Urgency

As you ask questions and get answers, watch for a sense of urgency—how motivated is the customer to take action? What is their level of desire to enjoy the benefits of the purchase? Observe their tone of voice, words, or intensity of responses to your reward and consequence questions. Their body language, facial expressions, or energy levels may tell you more than their words.

You may get an indication of their urgency by asking questions like these:

- What's your time frame for achieving your desired situation?
- What other factors are involved in selecting a new solution?
- What challenges might you face in this transition?
- How can we help you make a smooth transition?

Don't Worry If You Don't Bat 1,000

Life gives us all chances to learn not only from our successes, but also from our failures. None of us is perfect. I've never applied the six-step system perfectly. Nor do I expect to do so. But I do try to learn each time I misapply it.

One of my biggest flops was several years ago when I called on the director of human resources and training of one of the three largest life insurance company home offices in New York City. It was the same company that I mentioned in Chapter 2, only thirteen years later, and I was visiting a person in a different position.

One of their regional managers had conducted my course and had experienced great results in increased sales. She had obtained the appointment for me at 2:00 on a Friday.

So I flew to New York and got into the person's office at 1:45. So 2:00 came, 2:15, 2:30, 2:45, 3:00, and finally at about 3:15 he came into the office. He looked at me and said, "What in the hell are you doing in my office?" At first I thought he was joking, and I said something smart-aleck back to him. Then I found out in no uncertain terms that he wasn't kidding.

He was a thin, sour old man, with a blue serge suit that had too many miles on its speedometer, along with too many bushels of dandruff all over his shoulders.

He sat down and asked me what I wanted. I told him about the work we did in the southeast region. He wanted to know who'd approved it, knowing full well who had, as the regional manager had set up my appointment with him. Undoubtedly, she'd told him of her success with our course.

For the next thirty minutes he reamed me out for bothering him and told me that they had no interest in anything that I had to offer them.

I was shell-shocked at his nastiness. I wanted to ask if he had enough money for counseling, or if he'd suffered abuse as a child. Did his father love him? Did his mother nurse him too long? Was he potty-trained too late in his childhood? Did his third-grade teacher slap his hands for coloring outside the lines?

But I finally decided that my questions might be too intrusive and break up the warm, fuzzy rapport we'd built.

Finally he asked, "Why do you think we'd be interested in your program?"

Knowing that I was going nowhere, I replied, "Because your people told us that it was much better than your current sales training." I assumed he wanted to know the truth.

Well, he pulled himself up, and I thought he was going to reach across the table and pop me. Then he proudly said, "I wrote our current program!"

I looked at him, took a deep breath, and said: "Then that would explain why it isn't very good." (Well, this is what I wanted to say, but in retrospect what I actually said was probably something nicer.)

Having said that, I got up, put everything back in my briefcase, and walked out.

Good lesson in the realities, not the logic, of selling. Egos and political positions reign supreme in many contacts.

LISTEN Self-Assessment

Please read each statement and ask yourself, "How descriptive is this statement of my actual behaviors with clients?" If it's always descriptive, circle 10; if it's never descriptive, circle 1; if it's sometimes descriptive, circle the appropriate number in between.

1. I always make sure I've connected and gained rapport with people before I begin my LISTEN diagnostic questions.

    1   2   3   4   5   6   7   8   9   10

2. My purpose is always to gather information that helps me understand people's current and desired situations in order to see if they need my help.

    1   2   3   4   5   6   7   8   9   10

3. I always involve all the decision makers in this diagnostic step.

    1   2   3   4   5   6   7   8   9   10

4. I carefully plan the questions I will ask a client during this step.

    1   2   3   4   5   6   7   8   9   10

5. During this step my customers know that my objective is to understand their situations, and not just to sell them something.

1   2   3   4   5   6   7   8   9   10

Total: _____

How to Prepare for a Successful LISTEN Step

Before making your calls or contacts, write on a pad or enter into your electronic device the following questions and your best answers. Or go to the Diagnostics section at the end of this book and follow the instructions for downloading a Pre-Call planning form.

1. What might their current situation be?
2. What could their desired situation be?
3. What rewards might they enjoy if I helped them reach their desired situation?
4. What possible consequences could occur if they don't enjoy their desired situation?
5. What specific questions can I ask them to understand these previous four questions?
6. What other information do I need to get to understand their needs?

Chances are you'll guess at which questions to ask, but the exercise will more fully prepare your mind for your LISTEN meeting.

Coaching Yourself on the LISTEN Step

When you've achieved the following objectives, you'll have completed the LISTEN Step:

1. Customers admit having conflicts between where they are now and where they'd like to be—their current and desired situations.
2. They've talked about the rewards they'd enjoy if the gaps are closed.
3. They've admitted what the consequences might be if they don't close the gaps.
4. They've expressed a desire for a solution and are willing to talk to you about one.

Review two or three contacts you've had in the past. Then determine how many of these four steps you completed with each contact. If you didn't complete all of them, which ones did you skip? Most of us get so eager to tell customers about our products or services that we jump to that too quickly.

Until you've completed all of these four objectives, you may be moving too quickly through the six steps.

How to Benefit the Most from This Chapter

The LISTEN Step is the central process for client-focused selling. Probably more selling takes place during this step than any other, although there appears to be no selling happening at all—at least in the old traditional sense of product-focused selling that involved persuasion and convincing strategies.

This step is the major fulcrum, or lever, that supports the whole client-focus process. It's the piece that shows your professionalism. Heightens your trust levels with clients. Separates you from competitors. Positions you as a counselor. When done right, it gets your customers selling themselves.

The Diagnostic Conflict Model gets people discovering their own needs or desires, or problems they want solved. As they talk and you listen, you put them in the driver's seat. They then steer their own minds and thoughts into the discovery process.

To gain the most this week, please take the following actions:

1. Spend a week reading and reviewing this chapter.
2. Write the four LISTEN actions on an index card or your electronic device.
3. Apply these actions as often as you have opportunity.
4. Evaluate your practice against the points given in the Coaching Yourself on the LISTEN Step section.
5. Meet with your study group this week. Share how you applied the actions this week, what happened when you did, and what results you enjoyed.

Remember this fundamental fact: People purchase things only when there's a gap between where they are now and where they'd like to be. It's then the weight of the rewards versus the costs, and the consequences of not enjoying the rewards, that motivates their decisions. For some people, it's the consequences that motivate them the most. Others are moved to buy more for the rewards. In other words, the pain of the problem outweighs the cost of the cure, or vice versa. It's necessary to listen and understand which of these dominates each of your customer's decisions.

How to Transition to the ILLUSTRATE Step

Once your clients have admitted a conflict between where they are now and where they'd like to be, have talked about the rewards of resolving the conflict, and have explained the consequences of not taking action, it's time to get more information or do more fact-finding about the following:

- What problems, wants, needs, or solutions do they want to end up solving or enjoying?
- What are they replacing, now using, or wanting to change?
- What functions do they want to perform?
- What results do they want to achieve?

Once you've gathered enough information to fully understand what customers want to accomplish with their purchase, and if you believe you can give them the benefits they want, then it's time to transition to your ILLUSTRATE or presentation step. Your objective is to show and tell how the features of your product or service will give them the benefits they've told you they want to enjoy.

Depending on the size of the client's needs, you may have to spend time determining the proper solution. You'll want to consider these factors when making an appointment to get together again to present your recommendation to them. Or, of course, your sale may require less study and less time spent in working up your recommended solutions.

As often as you can, fill in a Post-Call planning form. You'll frequently make new discoveries about what you learned, or should have learned in your LISTEN Step. Filling in the form when your contact is fresh on your mind best prepares your next steps.

6

ILLUSTRATE

EXPLAINING HOW YOU CAN HELP CLIENTS ENJOY THEIR DESIRED BENEFITS

*But joy can be real only if people look upon their life
as a service, and have a definite object in life outside
themselves and their personal happiness.*

—LEO TOLSTOY

Most salespeople get it wrong.

They think people buy their products or services so they can have their products or services. They don't seem to know that customers want their products or services for the benefits they'll enjoy by having them, not always for what they are.

But Alice Baker, a real estate agent in Nashville, Tennessee, knows this difference. This helps her close a much higher than average percentage of homes for her potential clients. Alice recently had clients come from out of town. Before meeting her, they'd looked at several homes and still hadn't found what they wanted. Rather than beginning by showing homes, she asked to get to know them. Sitting down with them, she asked questions about their lifestyle, family, entertainment, and other activities and functions. One of the questions she asked the couple was, "Is there a *most important thing* about the home you want?"

"Yes, there is," they replied. They named a specific school district they wanted their children to attend. Alice then checked in two subdivisions that were close to the schools and found out that there were no homes listed in the price range that they wanted to pay.

So she sent out letters to all the people in these two subdivisions, asking if anyone wanted to sell their home. Immediately, she got four calls from people who were willing to sell. She looked at the four homes before showing them to her clients, carefully analyzing their features to see which one would best suit them, based on their conversations. Those were mainly a gourmet kitchen, four bedrooms, and a large lot.

Alice showed her potential clients the first home that she felt would best serve their needs. She carefully explained how each of the home's features would address the lifestyle and family needs they'd previously expressed. She explained each feature with the words, "Here's how this will help you enjoy . . ." and then mentioned the benefits they had told her they wanted the home to provide for them. In other words, she fit the features of the home to their admitted wants, needs, or lifestyle—giving them the quality of life they'd told her they wanted to achieve.

They bought the home she showed them.

Alice had learned years before that people don't buy the features of homes; rather they buy for how the features will provide for them the quality of life they'll enjoy.

Tie Everything Back to People's
Wants or Needs

In client-focused selling we never ILLUSTRATE, or tell about our products or services, until we've completed the LISTEN Step. Don't move to this step until you understand people's wants, needs, problems, or goals, and believe you have the best solution for them.

Why Do People Buy Your Product or Service?

Simple question, isn't it? But a very important one. Here's where many salespeople stray from being client-focused. They quickly become product-focused. Go look at a home that's for sale, or an automobile. How do the salespeople begin their conversations? Usually by saying something like, "It's got three thousand square feet, three bedrooms, and a two-car garage, and the owner is motivated to sell." They assume that they're selling houses, not fitting a home to your wants, needs, or lifestyle.

Several years ago I went into a dealership to look at a new Mercedes. As I was drooling over it, a salesperson came up to me and his first words were, "It's got seventy pounds of paint on it." When he said that, I thought, *I am so relieved to know it has seventy pounds on it, I was in a near panic state, afraid it only had sixty-eight pounds.* He then popped the hood and told me about the cubic centimeters of displacement the engine offered. He didn't seem to notice that my need to know was the color, how fast the car would go, and how fast could I buy it.

Here's the point: People aren't so interested in what your product or service *is*; rather they're concerned about what it will *do* for them. The benefits they'll enjoy. How it will help them:

- Look good
- Feel better
- Live longer
- Get ahead of their neighbors
- Earn more
- Have a happy family
- Feel financially secure
- Get a promotion
- Impress others

These are some of the reasons why people buy—many of which aren't logical at all.

It's taken me almost forty years to get up the courage to admit this, but I once bought a new Mercedes because I was making a speech for an upscale Junior League audience. I wanted to impress them with my success, should any of them see what kind of car I drove. Which they probably didn't. And, more than likely, they couldn't have cared less. But the Mercedes salesman still made a sale that day.

Basic Buying Motives

There are four dominant buying motives:

1. Pride—pride of ownership
2. Profit—to increase, gain, save, earn
3. Pleasure—enjoyment, entertainment, fun, social activity
4. Peace—peace of mind; freedom from worry, risk, or problems

You'll notice that these seem to correlate with the four Personality Patterns.

- Pleasure fits a Socializer
- Pride fits an Achiever
- Profit fits a Controller
- Peace fits a Conformer

Obviously, since people are more complex, these aren't always exact match-ups. I only mention them as general types and patterns to observe.

CLIENT-Focused Sales System

Step 3. ILLUSTRATE: Explaining How You Can Help Clients Enjoy Their Desired Benefits

The following actions will help you share how your product features will help customers enjoy the benefits they admitted desiring in your LISTEN Step. So your conversation is not just about what your product or services are, but how they'll deliver the benefits that your customers told you they wanted.

ILLUSTRATE Actions to Practice

1. Refer back to their admitted wants or needs.
2. Explain your features and benefits that will satisfy their wants or needs.
3. Ask for feedback throughout your presentation.
4. Present the price at the right time.

Take a moment and write these on an index card or your electronic device, so you have them handy and can refer to them frequently each day.

ACTION 1. REFER BACK TO THEIR ADMITTED WANTS OR NEEDS

This may occur at the same meeting when you completed your LIS-TEN Step, or at a rescheduled one. It's good to first gain rapport and then take a moment and review the desired situations your customers said they wanted to enjoy from their purchase. Often these desires change when time has gone by. Or, with more rapport, deeper reasons for the purchase can surface.

Your review might go something like this: "Let me make sure I understood what you're looking for in a new home. You want a bedroom for each of your three children, a kitchen and den combination for entertaining, fireplaces in both the den and living room, and a patio that faces south for morning sun. And your price range is approximately three hundred thousand dollars. What else did you tell me that I need to remember?"

By following these guidelines, you'll stay client-focused. You'll show that your focus is helping them enjoy the benefits they told you they want. This demonstrates your desire to help them and not just sell to them. Trust intensifies with your sincere desire to help them.

ACTION 2. EXPLAIN YOUR FEATURES AND BENEFITS THAT WILL SATISFY THEIR WANTS OR NEEDS

Your product may have a dozen good features, but your client may be interested in only one or two. You'll want to discover those in your

LISTEN Step and focus on them in your presentation, and not the "seventy pounds of paint." Avoid going on and on about features that excite you, unless they also excite your clients.

"Here's How This Will Help You"

These are the six magic words that will help you make the feature/benefit conversion. When mentioning a feature, you follow it with, "Here's how this will help you." Then tell customers how it will give them a benefit they admitted wanting to achieve.

This is a way to stay client-focused.

Remember, people don't just buy product or service features—even the latest, greatest electronic technology; they buy for *how the features will benefit them.* Their perceived benefits can range from the usage of the new technology to keeping up with their crowd in having the latest and greatest.

As obvious as this sounds, few salespeople either know or do this.

These six magic words can work magic for you.

ACTION 3. ASK FOR FEEDBACK THROUGHOUT YOUR PRESENTATION

You'll want to make your ILLUSTRATE Step as interactive as possible. You can do this by asking for feedback throughout your presentation. You'll do half of the talking and half of the listening in your presentation. Your clients will fill their half of the conversation by giving you feedback about their understanding, opinions, and responses.

As you mention specific features, ask feedback questions like the following:

- What do you think of this feature?
- What more can I explain?
- How do you see this solving your problem or satisfying your requirements?
- What question do you have about this?
- What benefits do you see this giving you?

Listen to how they respond, their tone of voice, and their body language. As your trust and rapport increases, you may pick up on objections they haven't mentioned yet. It's not uncommon for Socializers and Conformers to withhold objections, so you may have to dig them out.

It's natural for salespeople to not welcome negative responses from clients. When you hear objections you may try to prove them wrong, creating a conflict that can block further communication. So as not to break rapport with people, when you do get negative feedback, you should welcome it, and ask for clarification. You can do this with questions like, "Thank you for sharing that; help me understand that more." Often, in explaining their negative or positive responses to your presentation, people will talk themselves out of their negativity. When they verbalize their thinking, and you listen objectively, they may realize their concerns aren't as important as they had stated.

Many salespeople make their product presentations a monologue rather than a two-way conversation. Avoid this. Ask questions. Seek to understand. Strive to see the world through your clients' eyes.

Keeping your purpose statement in mind at all times during your presentation will cause you to stay focused on your objective of delivering the most benefits to the most people.

Levels of Benefits People May Want

People can often be motivated to buy things for reasons that they don't want to admit or that aren't based on logic, and you have to dig their feelings or objections out. Look for deeper motivations, such as the following:

- To make themselves look good.
- To keep themselves from looking bad.
- For self-preservation.
- To please others.
- To repay friendships.
- To keep up with the crowd.
- To avoid risks.
- To protect their own egos.

Of course, you can't intuitively know all these reasons, but you can be on the lookout for them, aware they may exist.

The largest sale I ever made was to Chevrolet. We had around 28,000 salespeople go through my Integrity Selling Course the first year. I first assumed they bought the course to satisfy dealer demand and help their salespeople sell more. I found out later that their main reason was to quiet a growing growling from women's groups for better treatment when they went into dealerships.

Apparently, the word *integrity* made the sale for me.

ACTION 4. PRESENT THE PRICE AT THE RIGHT TIME

Here's a sales principle worth remembering: Your price is important only after people have agreed that your product or service will give them the benefits they want. Until this point, the price is irrelevant.

The right time to present the price is when the customer has said, "Yes, I like what you've presented, and believe it will give me the benefits I want; how much will it cost?"

Handling Premature Price Questions

However, the customer often may begin asking for prices before you ever get to the appropriate time to deal with them. Here's a response you can give them when they ask premature price questions.

1. "I understand your concern about the price. I know that you want to get the best price possible."
2. "But before I can give you an exact price, there's some more information I need," or
3. "Before I can give you an exact price, let's make sure we've selected the best solution for you."

After saying this, ask for the information you need to get.

Present the Price with Confidence

When it's the right time to present the price, follow these suggestions:

1. Look directly into the client's eyes, or mentally look at them through the telephone, and don't look away.
2. Confidently quote the price, believing that your product or service is worth much more than what you're asking.
3. Emphasize the benefits the client will enjoy.

When you're convinced that the value exceeds the cost, you'll communicate that in your demeanor, eye contact, and voice. Before you discuss price with your customer, be ready to mention several ways that your service will exceed the price you'll ask for it. Convince yourself first, then the client. This is a critical point, as you can unconsciously fear clients' forthcoming objections to the price, and even invite them if you present the price weakly and unconvincingly.

However, a lot of buyers are preconditioned to object to the price, no matter what it is.

So what do you do in that situation?

A Vulnerable Moment

For a great lesson in human behavior, the next ten times you ask the price of an item you're thinking about purchasing, notice what salespeople do with their eyes when they mention the price. Chances are most of them will look away or down when they say it. What does that tell you?

You can be confident and have good rapport with customers until it comes time to present the price, and suddenly things can get sticky. How you handle this moment of truth can shade your relationship throughout the rest of the sales process. There's another potential problem involved here. When you're afraid that people will respond negatively to your price, it can influence the way you say it. Your fear can even be subliminally communicated to your customers, causing them to have inner doubts about the wisdom of this purchase.

Make sure you believe the benefits you give clients will significantly outweigh the cost to them, and confidently look into their eyes when you quote your price.

Should buyers want what you're offering but want to argue over the price, you might get agreement from them that this is what they want, except for the price. Then, if this is appropriate in your business, you might ask what their budget is. Your organization probably has specific negotiation policies.

Presenting to Different Personality Patterns

Depending on your own Personality Pattern, as well as your customers', here are some suggestions that will help you connect with them during the ILLUSTRATE Step:

- *Achievers:* Talk in terms of results, the bottom line, and achievement. Keep your presentation short, emphasizing the main results they'll enjoy. Don't get too wrapped up in details, but let them know that you'll take care of their needs.
- *Socializers:* Talk about how this purchase will make them look good to others, and how they will enjoy owning your product or service. Show them you're a friend who cares about them.
- *Conformers:* Give lots of details about how things work and what to do if things go wrong. Take as much pressure off them as possible. Expect them to take more time and move slowly when accepting new ideas. Don't present ideas that require too much change on their part. Minimize risks.
- *Controllers:* Talk to them in logical terms. They'll show little emotion and will not give you as much feedback as Socializers or Achievers. They'll be more critical in evaluating your presentation and demand more proof or evidence to support your claims.

ILLUSTRATE Self-Assessment

Please read each statement and ask yourself, "How descriptive is this statement of my actual behaviors with clients?" If it's always descriptive, circle 10; if it's never descriptive, circle 1; if it's sometimes descriptive, circle the appropriate number in between.

1. I never talk about my product or service until clients have admitted a want or need that I can help them satisfy.

   1 2 3 4 5 6 7 8 9 10

2. I carefully tell how my product features will give customers the benefits they admitted wanting.

   1 2 3 4 5 6 7 8 9 10

3. I am always careful to understand each person's Personality Patterns and fit my benefit statements to them.

   1 2 3 4 5 6 7 8 9 10

4. I always try to do half of the talking and half of the listening, by asking for feedback as I make my presentations.

   1 2 3 4 5 6 7 8 9 10

5. Before presenting the price of my solutions, I have always established how the value far exceeds the cost.

   1 2 3 4 5 6 7 8 9 10

   Total: _____

How to Prepare for a Successful ILLUSTRATE Step

This step may be done in the same meeting as your CONNECT and LISTEN Steps, or it might be after multiple meetings. Whichever it is, you'll need to prepare for it:

- Write down the two or three major benefits your customers want to enjoy or achieve.
- Write out specific ways your solutions will give them the benefits they want to enjoy.
- Sell yourself on the value you'll give them above their costs.
- Think about possible concerns your clients might have that they haven't brought up before, and prepare responses to those concerns.
- Tailor the description of your product's benefits to your customers' Personality Patterns.

Coaching Yourself on the ILLUSTRATE Step

You've completed this step when:

1. Customers understand your recommendation and believe it will fill their wants or needs.
2. Their questions and concerns have been successfully answered.
3. Everyone who has decision influence has been included in your presentation.

4. You've identified any roadblocks or concerns they may have about making decisions.

Until these points have been successfully accomplished, your clients may not have enough belief in the value of your solutions to make decisions. While you may not know this now, you may find it out in your EVALUATE Step.

How to Benefit the Most from This Chapter

As your "Print Coach," allow me to play a "mother's role" and emphasize again the value of practicing the concepts I write about. Just reading them will do you little good. Knowledge is only power as it's practiced.

To gain the most from this chapter, read it again, and then come back and do the following:

1. Select one or two actions on which to focus your practice in your actual selling activities.
2. Take a few minutes at the beginning of the week and score yourself on the ILLUSTRATE Self-Assessment.
3. Select one statement from your self-assessment that you'd like to strengthen, and take action to do so.
4. Evaluate yourself on the four Coaching Yourself points to determine the ones you have or haven't completed.
5. Attend your weekly study group, sharing how you practiced the ILLUSTRATE actions, what happened when you practiced them, what you learned, and how it will help you sell more.

Just as a coach gets his or her athletic team out on the field each day—practicing, practicing, practicing—you can follow the same successful process.

Daily Success Conditioning Forms

Let me once more remind you to keep a stack of Daily Success Conditioning forms, referred to in the Diagnostics section of this book. Fill one out at the end of each day. This only takes five minutes, and is a powerful way to reinforce your CLIENT-focused thinking and habits.

Sustained daily use of it eventually creates strong, positive emotions of confidence and eager anticipation to see as many people as you can to see who needs your help.

Separate Yourself

The ILLUSTRATE Step separates you from most other people who still do transaction- or product-focused selling. They still make their features their selling levers, rather than the *value* these features provide their customers. Your client focus causes you to speak a different language than people who do other types of selling. Your selling purpose is also different, as it's the image you cast with clients. When people get the message that you want to help them, rather than sell to them, your relationships will be transformed. They'll want to buy from you.

How to Transition to the EVALUATE Step

During your EVALUATE Step, you find out if new objections or challenges develop, and you reinforce and communicate the value your clients will enjoy. Once you think you have completed the ILLUSTRATE Step, your transition might go something like this:

> "If you don't mind, before we go further, let's take a moment, review the benefits you wanted to enjoy, and make sure we've selected the best solutions for you."

Obviously, you do this to the level of the sale you're making. The more complex the sale, the more you'll want to do it. But you can do it even with small sales. Strong trust is built when you sincerely carry out this step.

7

EVALUATE

MAKING SURE YOUR SOLUTIONS ARE RIGHT FOR CLIENTS

Do the right thing because it's the right thing to do.

—W. CLEMENT STONE

Evaluating, a seeming nonselling step, is actually a powerful selling strategy.

That's why Bill Gregg, a successful dentist in Laguna Niguel, California, has such high patient satisfaction scores. After putting people at ease, he engages them in very friendly conversation while he examines them to determine what their dental needs are, how they feel about the state of their teeth now, and what they'd like for their dental health to be. Then he carefully plans out the work he thinks a patient needs, and presents it to them. After getting agreement that the work he prescribes is what they want, he builds models that show the completed work. That's what he did for me. We scheduled the work, and it was completed.

Fast-forward a couple of months.

Very early on a Sunday morning he sent me an email wanting to know how my dental work was holding up. Why would a dentist take time at five a.m. on a Sunday morning to check on the work he did for me two months ago? Easy answer if you knew Bill—*he cares*. He genuinely wanted to know how happy I was with his treatment.

Bill embodies the *Soul* of selling, or serving, in the work he does. Strong values, genuine interest in the welfare of his patients, and deep sincerity define who he is. More than seeing what he does as "fixing teeth," he stretches past that and views himself as contributing to patients' quality of life. He's very diligent about helping people look good and feel good as a result of his dental work. Is it any wonder that although he's tried to retire, his old patients keep him in business?

I don't know this to be a fact, but I'm guessing that because of his sincere desire to help people, he gets much less quibbling about his fees than other dentists do. And I'm also sure that his patient satisfaction levels are much higher than most others. He embodies the old saying, "At the end of every tooth is a person."

We Usually Get Back What We Give Out

Before we go further, let's examine a formidable law of human action: *the law of psychological reciprocity*. As suggested by the heading, this law means that *we get back what we give out*. People are psychologically impelled to return to us the same attitudes and responses that we give to them.

"Does this always work?" you ask. No, not always, as some people are so self-focused that they're incapable of giving back, but they're in a minority.

One way to trigger this reciprocity is to give *psychological value* to clients. We do this by first sincerely valuing them as God-created human beings. By listening to and understanding them. By reinforcing the positive responses we receive from them, and understanding why they might have negative ones. Thanking them. Expressing positive beliefs in them. Sincerely agreeing with them when we can. Giving them rewarding remarks. Paraphrasing the responses they give us to show we understand them.

But it's not easy for many salespeople to do what I call *listen to understand*. Most people tend to *listen to agree or disagree*. Think about this for a moment. One of a client's strongest personal needs is to be understood. Their silent cry is, "Please understand me. Understand what I'm saying, how I feel, who I am, what I think."

They'll often forgo some of their demands if they believe you truly want to understand their position and viewpoint. Customers have a need to defend their positions, and the more we attempt to change their minds, the more they become rigid in holding on to their opinions.

When you sincerely want to help people get the most value for their purchase, the EVALUATE Step will communicate that, and they'll get the message. When you show your interest in and understanding of them, most people will return these values to you by trusting you, being more open to understanding your solutions, and wanting to buy from you.

The Purpose of the EVALUATE Step

- It gives you a chance to double-check to make sure you've understood the client's objectives.
- It gives you feedback and lets you know if any concerns remain unanswered.
- It gets the client talking and confirming their needs and the efficacy of your solutions.
- It gets customers mentally and emotionally reliving the benefits that would come with a purchase.

- It cements trust and causes people to want to do business with you.

As you accomplish these objectives, you'll draw your clients closer to you, and you'll do something that few of your competitors know to do.

Not Always a Natural Behavior

Your natural reaction when you've finished a successful presentation is to go for a close—hoping people will buy before they think of new reasons not to do so. The EVALUATE Step not only gives you a chance to see if they're really sold, but it also provides a way to help customers resell themselves.

John Cato was having a difficult time understanding the power of the EVALUATE Step—until, during a client contact, it clicked in his mind that after he'd completed the CONNECT, LISTEN, and ILLUSTRATE Steps, his prospect still seemed confused and didn't understand all the technology involved. Sensing this, John asked, "To make sure my solution is the best one for you, do you mind if we take a couple of minutes and review what we've discussed to this point, just to make sure I'm recommending the best solution for you?"

His prospect was a broker who'd never done business with John's company and was not technologically educated to understand John's systems. After John applied the EVALUATE Step, the client handed the proposal back to him and said, "I still don't understand all this, but I trust you, so let's go with it."

John's commission was approximately $300,000.

Few salespeople, especially Achievers, take the time to perform this step. Maybe they just don't know to do it. Maybe they are too eager to close the sale. Or maybe they don't want to open themselves up to the possibility of new concerns or objections. So they miss a great opportunity to cement relationships and complete more transactions.

Another benefit of the EVALUATE Step is to keep different people in the loop who are involved in a purchase decision but can't all be in the same meetings. Or maybe the person with whom you're dealing needs more confidence in your proposal before they're comfortable taking it to higher decision makers or influencers. You'll also want to adjust your evaluation to the Personality Patterns of the buyers. I'll write more about this in a few moments.

You may be thinking, "Why should I give people a chance to bring up more objections?" The reason is that if they do exist, and if you don't deal with them here, they'll probably come up later. And "later" may be after you've had a chance to deal with them.

Here are the EVALUATE actions to practice this week.

CLIENT-Focused Sales System

Step 4. EVALUATE: Making Sure Your Solutions Are Right for Clients

EVALUATE Actions to Practice

1. Review clients' desired benefits.
2. Show how they will enjoy extra value above the cost.
3. Find out what concerns remain unanswered.
4. Address concerns.

Let's think about each of these actions.

ACTION 1. REVIEW CLIENTS' DESIRED BENEFITS

You might introduce this part by saying, "Before we move on, let's take a few moments and review what you want to accomplish with your purchase, and make sure that I've recommended the best solution for you."

I first learned this lesson many years ago when, out of college, I was selling office equipment and had a department store client who wanted to replace their counters. I measured everything and could tell that the manager was a bit reluctant to trust my ability to get the measurements accurately. So I called Roy Klein, our factory representative in Dallas. He complimented me for selling the equipment and suggested that he fly in and double-check all the measurements. My customer was very impressed that he would fly in just to make sure everything was correctly measured.

Mr. Klein was a very dignified gentleman, exuding an aura of honesty, sincerity, and respectability that caused people to immediately trust him. He remeasured the dimensions and reviewed the style, finish, and costs with the store manager. The sale was quickly consummated. The manager seemed to have much more confidence in me, and when the installation was completed, they began to purchase much more from me.

Saying, "Let's make sure this will be the best solution," or, "Let's make sure we get this right," are powerful ways to strengthen trust and relationships.

ACTION 2. SHOW HOW THEY WILL ENJOY
EXTRA VALUE ABOVE THE COST

Extra value can be anything that you give people beyond the actual benefits of your product or service. It might be emotional support, a fun activity, or a thoughtful gesture. The size of it doesn't always matter. The unexpected nature of it is usually what sticks out in your customers' minds.

There are many ways to show extra value. Back when I was selling office equipment, I competed against other salespeople who sold some of the same things I did. I looked for different ways to serve my customers and prove that I was the best person with whom to do business.

As I called on companies, I'd look for broken chairs and offer to take them back to the store and fix them, while lending my customers new ones. Most of the time, the customers purchased the loaners because they were so much more comfortable. I'd offer to review clients' filing or billing systems and often found that they needed updated ones. Many of my customers took me out for coffee and "got stuff off their chests." I had people tell me about their problems with their children, co-workers, cars, or other things. I got most of a hospital's business by taking the purchasing agent out to the firing range on Saturdays.

I didn't understand the word *lagniappe* then, but I understood its concept—*a little something extra*.

Remember, it's the unexpected nature of it that sticks in your customers' minds.

ACTION 3. FIND OUT WHAT CONCERNS REMAIN UNANSWERED

While it's normal to dodge bad news, if we leave concerns unaddressed, we may lose sales and never realize why. Client concerns, problems, or objections can be dealt with only when we ask for and understand them.

A good question to ask at this point in a meeting is, "Do you have any other questions or concerns that we should think about?" This is a much easier question to ask when you're truly client-focused than when you're just trying to make a sale. Your sincerity in asking has a silent power in strengthening trust with your clients.

When you get responses, to let your customer know that you truly want to work out any issues, you might thank them and ask, "Please help me understand that." When you openly ask for more information so you can understand their concerns, you have a chance to respond without seeming to be combative. Also, you strengthen your rapport with them.

Should you discover they don't want to work their concerns out, you may be at the end of the road. Hopefully, though, the client should be willing to address their concerns with you, so you need to find out what action they want to take now.

ACTION 4. ADDRESS CONCERNS

When clients do want to work out concerns they may have, it's appropriate to ask for their opinions about the best way to proceed. Put the ball back in their court; ask for their opinions about the best solutions. Don't be too quick in giving them your opinions. Remember, people are more apt to act upon their suggestions, rather than yours.

When people do express their negative feelings or concerns, show that you understand them. Openly listen. Avoid closed body language like folded arms, frowning, backing away from them, or other signs that you don't agree with them. Most importantly, don't interrupt. Simply listen. Unless you have very strong rapport and trust with people, it's best not to try to prove them wrong—even when they are.

Remember the law of psychological reciprocity—we tend to get back from people the same feelings and attitudes we give out to them. So give positive feedback to people whether their responses are positive or negative. You can do this by saying, "I understand," or, "I see what you mean." Show your understanding of their thinking. Then paraphrase or summarize back to them your understanding of their responses. This is a positive way to keep customers from closing their mental gates and locking you out.

When people trust you and feel comfortable with you, and you think of a solution, you might say something like, "May I offer a suggestion?" When you get permission, you might say, "What do you think of this idea?" Persuasive tactics tend to block trust at this point. Listening and understanding tend to open up communication channels.

From Persuasion to Helping People Change Their Minds

Let's change the word *persuasion* to *helping people change their minds*. It's not something we persuade people to do; it's something they want to do, because the benefits outweigh the costs. Big difference. This kicks the old manipulative "overcoming stalls and objections" sales strategies out the door.

Great salespeople have learned that helping people change their minds is achieved more by social interaction than one-way monologues. *Social interaction* is the process by which people influence one another through their mutual interchange of thoughts, feelings, and reactions. It's about conversational give and take. Here are some actions that contribute to social interaction:

- Soliciting opinions
- Nodding approval to prove your understanding
- Paraphrasing or summarizing what you heard

- Asking for clarification
- Understanding
- Reinforcement

These communication concepts apply from your CONNECT Step through the end of your contacts. The EVALUATE Step also gives you an excellent time to use them. When your genuine desire is to understand and create win-win exchanges of value, you'll subliminally communicate that to your clients, and they'll be receptive to that intent.

Perceived Value Is the Major Motivator

People are mainly motivated by perceived value. You can begin to understand what each person perceives as value in your LISTEN Step. Then as the sales process goes along, you'll probably learn more about what your customers believe to be the main value for them. Much of the time this is discovered indirectly, as people can have some crazy reasons for buying things and often won't admit the real reasons until stronger rapport is established.

I've lost sales to companies because I was presenting and relying on logic and value, and the buyers were looking through the lenses of their own political positions.

So do what I call *listening sideways*. Listen from the peripheries for what people are meaning but not saying. What are they telling you with their body language that's different from the words they're using?

Open-ended questions can help you understand what the client's perceived value is:

- Tell me more about what you're thinking.
- Who else will be involved in the benefits of your purchase?
- What other things do you need to consider before making a decision?
- What will you enjoy (financially, physically, emotionally) if you make this purchase?
- What are some possible risks you might run in making a purchase decision?
- What personal goals do you have that I might help you reach?

Without admitting it, most corporate purchasers are thinking, "How will this purchase decision affect me?"

Inner Conflicts Drive Decisions

The EVALUATE Step gives you another chance to get people thinking through their current and desired situations, hopefully arousing a *cognitive dissonance*.

Remember, before people make decisions there must be an *inner conflict* between where they are now and where they'd like to be— between what they have now and what they'd like to have. What they are not enjoying now and what they'd like to be enjoying.

You discovered some of these conflicts in your LISTEN Step as you took people through the Diagnostic Conflict Model. You'll want to try to discover more about the conflicts they are experiencing and the relative power of those conflicts. From your LISTEN Step until now, time has gone by, and the conflicts may have become more intense as your clients have gone through the thinking process through which you've taken them.

Should discussions stall during the EVALUATE Step, you'll most often discover it's because you didn't totally finish the Diagnostic Conflict Model in the LISTEN Step. Revisit the earlier step by saying, "I'm not sure I fully understood your desired situation . . . may I ask some more questions that help me understand it more completely?" You may need to discover more about how their desired rewards outweigh their costs and how their feared consequences outweigh the risks of not buying. When you can bring these into a tighter focus, you'll help people make easier decisions.

EVALUATE Self-Assessment

Please read each statement and ask yourself, "How descriptive is this statement of my actual behaviors with clients?" If it's always descriptive, circle 10; if it's never descriptive, circle 1; if it's sometimes descriptive, circle the appropriate number in between.

1. I always take time to make sure what I'm recommending is the best value for my clients.

   1 2 3 4 5 6 7 8 9 10

2. I sincerely want to understand my clients' opinions and concerns at this point of the sale.

   1 2 3 4 5 6 7 8 9 10

3. I always ask questions to determine what clients are thinking at this point.

   1 2 3 4 5 6 7 8 9 10

4. I always want to know the truth, even though it may not be favorable for me.

    1   2   3   4   5   6   7   8   9   10

5. I'm always careful to give positive reinforcement to clients regardless of the responses I get from them.

    1   2   3   4   5   6   7   8   9   10

Total: _____

Adjusting to Different Personality Patterns

Keeping in mind how your own Personality Patterns will interact with other people's patterns is especially important in the EVALUATE Step, as this is the point of nearing a purchase decision. Here are some points to remember when performing this step with clients of different patterns:

- *Socializers* want you to like and accept them. Unless the purchase is a personal item, they may need others to help them make decisions. Find out whom they want to please or impress with the purchase. Focus on the relationship benefits they'll enjoy because of the purchase. Minimize the risks. Maximize the rewards they'll enjoy, as the hope of reward motivates them more than the fear of risks.
- *Achievers* make quick decisions and stick with them. They want to see how the bottom line will be strengthened. They don't want you telling them what to

do, and they will resist any pressure, as it takes away from their need for power. They must see how purchasing your solutions will make them look stronger and more successful. This is more important to them and overpowers most of the risks involved.

- *Conformers* need security and reassurance. Being risk averse, they'll need to believe that their risk will be minimized. Take your time with them, as they make slow decisions. Show them how your solutions are "tried and true." They are motivated more by removal of risk than by hope of reward.

- *Controllers* won't give you much feedback. They want accurate, logical, validated information. They are decisive when they have all the facts and logically see that the benefits outweigh the costs of your products or services. You must be factual and even understate your benefits. They like "devil's advocates." Bring up the potential weaknesses before mentioning the strong positives.

Coaching Yourself on the EVALUATE Step

As you focus on this step this week, check back and make sure you've accomplished these goals:

1. You reviewed what your clients wanted to achieve and the benefits they want to enjoy.
2. You secured agreement again that this is what they want to achieve.
3. They have no more questions or concerns.

4. They agreed that the value you can give them is worth more than the cost.

Remember to travel at the emotional speed of your clients' patterns, and not that of your own.

How to Prepare for This Session

Always enter your contacts by rethinking how your customers will enjoy specific benefits that exceed their costs. When you have time, write these out and visualize your customers enjoying them. Often, when it's time for your EVALUATE Step, having finished the ILLUSTRATE Step in the same visit, your recall will be more effective when you've reviewed their benefits.

Also, when you're focused on what your clients will enjoy from their purchase, rather than what you'll get out of it, you'll communicate that to them on a deep unconscious level.

How to Benefit the Most from This Chapter

As in the preceding chapters, please focus on opportunities to apply the four EVALUATE actions. Of course, you'll continue to apply the other client-focused steps as situations present themselves.

Here are some suggestions for gaining the most from this chapter.

1. Keep the six CLIENT-Focused Sales System steps handy.
2. Review them each day.

3. Evaluate how well you practiced them after contacts, and think about how you can apply them more effectively.

4. Continue benefiting from the Pre-Call and Post-Call forms (see the Diagnostics section of this book for download instructions).

5. Fill in the EVALUATE Self-Assessment, and select one statement that you want to strengthen.

6. Keep repeating your client-focused purpose statement that you composed in Chapter 1. Allow it to be your elevator speech—whenever someone asks you what you do, repeat your purpose speech.

7. Meet with your study group this week.

How to Transition to the NEGOTIATE Step

After you've successfully completed your EVALUATE Step, it's time to go to your NEGOTIATE Step. You can ask, "Is there anything else we need to discuss before we finalize the transaction?" Or "Where are we now in the decision process?" Or "What else do we need to discuss for you to make a decision?"

If the customer gives you reason to believe they're ready to buy, proceed to the TRANSACT Step. But sometimes you discover that they still have issues that need to be worked through. Few sales go perfectly. This is when you go to the NEGOTIATE Step.

8

NEGOTIATE

WORKING OUT PROBLEMS THAT
KEEP CLIENTS FROM BUYING

If the Golden Rule is to be preached at all in these modern days,
when so much of our life is devoted to business, it must be
preached specially in its application to the conduct of business.

—F. S. SCHENCK

If it isn't right for them, it isn't right for you.

Jerry Colangelo has done more to rebuild downtown Phoenix than anyone else in the last four decades. His bold dreams and strong actions brought it back from empty, graffiti-covered buildings to a vibrant attraction for entertainment and business.

First, Jerry built the Phoenix Suns downtown arena, and then the giant Diamondbacks stadium. Can you imagine the hundreds of negotiations he had to make? Old buildings had to be purchased and demolished. Dozens of major contractors vied for business. There were zoning issues, city taxes, real estate scammers looking to get in on deals. Without question it was his negotiation skills that mainly contributed to the total transformation of the downtown.

After completion of the Diamondbacks stadium, his skill in

trading for elite players contributed to their doing the impossible for a startup team—winning the World Series over the vaunted New York Yankees. Just thinking of the quality players he acquired leaves us breathless: Randy Johnson, Curt Schilling, Jay Bell, and Luis Gonzalez, to name a few.

As chairman of the USA Basketball headquarters, he negotiated their move from Colorado Springs, Colorado, to Tempe, Arizona, and is building a $350 million project. This complex houses a 330-room Omni Hotel, a 30,000-square-foot conference center, 500 luxury apartments, and 200,000 square feet of office space. All this on ten and a half acres next to Arizona State University.

How much negotiation might that have taken?

An expert win-win negotiator, Jerry is honest, upright, strong, determined, and fair. He wants to get the best deal for his interests, as he should, but he knows it must be a win for all the people with whom he's dealing. He has high values. I attended a Bible study that he hosted for a dozen or so businesspeople at the Phoenix Country Club. One of our regular attendees was Joe Garagiola, the famous baseball player and retired NBC *Good Morning America* host.

Well, you and I will probably never reach the height of business negotiating Jerry has reached, but negotiating is still an important component of the sales process. Are you confident in your negotiating skills? How do you view it: as a method of working out challenges with customers that are mutually beneficial and win-win, or as a ploy you implement to get the best deal for yourself?

Authentic Negotiation Isn't Manipulation

I called a carpet cleaning company called Zero-Rez to come and give me an estimate to clean my carpet. I left my name on a recording, and soon a nice person called me back and asked me several questions about the number and sizes of rooms I wanted cleaned.

She insisted on giving me a price of $189, saying that there might be a slight adjustment up or down, depending on the actual size when the service person got here.

When Mitch, the service person, came, he measured the rooms, telling me that he wouldn't charge me for the master bedroom, master bathroom, and closet. He figured and figured, and finally told me the price would be $330. I was a bit surprised and asked him if he knew what the person at his office quoted me. He said, "Yes, one eighty-nine."

"Why is there such a big difference in your two prices?"

"She didn't know the actual measurements."

"But I gave her the number of rooms, and the approximate size of each one. Now you're telling me that you're not going to charge me for the master bedroom, bath, and closet—and it's still almost twice as much as she quoted me."

He figured more, finally saying that he'd cut it to $299. I said I'd pay him $275, if he included a silicone spray after he cleaned it. He had to think about that and finally agreed.

It was a disappointing experience. The people were very nice. Mitch was not adversarial, but I felt manipulated—which I was.

After Mitch left, I wondered how he felt on the inside doing manipulative tactics he was trained to do.

How to Know When to Proceed to the Negotiate Step

When things go smoothly through your CONNECT, LISTEN, ILLUSTRATE, and EVALUATE steps, customers are often ready to buy. You have:

- Gained rapport and trust.
- Understood customers' wants, needs, problems, or desired solutions.
- Created a conflict in their minds between what they now have and what they'd like to have.
- Shown them how your product or service will give them benefits they want.
- Understood any concerns they might have and dealt with them.
- Reviewed how the benefits of your offering will give the benefits they want.

When you've successively completed these steps, you'll usually make a sale. But not always. Sometimes your customers suddenly have new thoughts, concerns, or doubts. When faced with making a decision, you may even witness a change in a person's facial expressions, body language, or attitude toward you. In an extreme case, it may appear that they now see you as an enemy, no longer a friend. Their excitement about the benefits of owning your solution can suddenly be converted into fear of making a bad decision. The rewards they previously visualized and talked about can vaporize. Or they may suddenly think of some other concern or issue they want cleared up.

At this point, you need to move to the NEGOTIATION Step.

A Moment of Truth

There's another issue here that can influence the sale. Not only can your customers suddenly experience the fear of making a final decision, but you can suddenly develop a fear that they're not going to buy. Nearing this "moment of truth" about a customer's decision to say yes or no can cause some moments of fear or apprehension. Sometimes we'd rather not know than risk finding out they aren't going to buy. The more you need to make a sale, or the more you're afraid they won't buy, the more this moment of truth comes surging in.

Unconsciously, you may be saying to yourself through your feelings:

- I'm afraid they're going to say no.
- I'd rather not know what their decision is than ask and get rejected.

In these situations, your emotions, body language, facial expressions, or attitudes can quickly change. Suddenly, the warm, friendly, trusting environment shifts. These phenomena can be driven by various factors influencing your emotions:

- Being on a financial survival level.
- Feelings of unworthiness.
- Focusing more on your needs than on the value clients will enjoy.
- Not believing that the value of your offering exceeds the cost to your customers.
- High need for acceptance and fear of rejection.

These are common challenges for many salespeople.

Remember: Clients Also Experience Their Own Moments of Truth

When decision time comes about, many customers experience sudden fears or apprehension about making a final decision. Socializers and Conformers often focus more on the risks than on the rewards—often needing more time, validation, or reinforcement from you. You may not recognize their need if you're an Achiever, and you can easily compound their fears by pressing them for a decision.

Negotiation Is a Win-Win

Many negotiation seminars and books teach strategies and tactics to win at the negotiating game. I realize that many people are in adversarial situations and the fate of nations, hostages, or lives are at stake. For the sake of this discussion, let's stay focused on you and your customers, where your objective is a win-win, mutual sharing of benefits. This win-win objective is a value that drives client-focused behaviors.

CLIENT-Focused Sales System

Step 5. NEGOTIATE: Working Out Problems
That Keep Clients from Buying

NEGOTIATE Actions to Practice

1. Ask where the client is in their decision process.
2. Listen to their response and paraphrase back your understanding.

3. Identify specific concerns and get agreement that they want to solve them.

4. Ask their opinions for best solutions and seek a win-win resolution.

ACTION 1. ASK WHERE THE CLIENT IS IN THEIR DECISION PROCESS

Often when you've reached this point in the CLIENT-Focused Sales System, your customers have either told you or implied that they're ready to finalize the transaction. When you find yourself with this reality, you skip the NEGOTIATION Step and proceed straight to the TRANSACT Step.

Otherwise, when you think you've completed all the previous steps of the CLIENT-Focused Sales System and there seem to be no more questions, concerns, or challenges, it's time to ask this question: "Where are we in the decision process?" Actually, there are a number of ways of asking this question.

- "What questions do I need to answer before you can make a decision?"
- "What time frame do you have for making a decision?"
- "Have I dealt with all your concerns?"

ACTION 2. LISTEN TO THEIR RESPONSE AND PARAPHRASE BACK YOUR UNDERSTANDING

Whether the responses you receive are positive or negative, understand them and summarize your understanding of what your clients said. If they are suddenly reluctant to spend extra money on certain features of your product, for instance, you might paraphrase your understanding like this: "I understand how you feel; you're not sure if the extra features justify the added cost."

You increase your empathy and rapport with people when you genuinely listen, understand, and share your understanding to them. This is a very effective communication action that counselors use to reinforce their patients' statements. When you value other people's thoughts, statements, or opinions, you become more like them and bond more with them, as one of people's greatest needs is to be understood. Once you have established strong rapport with customers and they trust you, they'll tend to accept your advice and thinking. You become a trusted advisor.

A few years ago one of my course graduates, Larry Merritt, of Tom Jumper Chevrolet in Atlanta, went into the *Guinness Book of World Records* as having sold more retail automobiles than anyone in the history of that industry. Over twenty years he averaged selling 60 retail new cars per month—three a working day, 12,000 in twenty years. Contrast this with the average salesperson's sales of twelve vehicles a month.

I spent a day in his dealership and found Larry to be the antithesis of a stereotypical "car guy." Nice, sincere, quiet, respectful, all described the person I found.

In a business that probably has more head-to-head, customer-to-salesperson, hard negotiation than most other vocations, Larry was different. When I asked him the secret of his success, he replied, "I just try to do the best job for my customers and my dealer." His customers trusted him because he valued their opinions and cared about their needs, so there was very little haggling when the time came to discuss the price.

The stronger the trust is, the more smoothly the NEGOTIATION Step goes.

ACTION 3. IDENTIFY SPECIFIC CONCERNS AND GET AGREEMENT THAT THEY WANT TO SOLVE THEM

When concerns do come up and you understand them, you might ask questions like these:

- "Thank you for sharing that; would you mind helping me understand what you're thinking?"
- "Thank you; is this something you want to work out?"
- "What would need to be worked out to make you happy?"

Recently, I called on a company who had used my courses in the past about installing my new Authentic Salesperson Course. It would involve my treating them as my personal client, instead of having another of our representatives handle it. The question, or objection, came up: "Well, what if something happens to you; how do we know that you have people who can update the material?"

My first objective was to find out if this was their only concern and, if we could satisfy it, whether they would be ready to proceed with an agreement.

I prepared a letter sharing specific people who can do updates, and they seemed to be happy. We're in the process of getting buy-in from their field managers.

Often when people believe you really want to understand them, their real issues come out that they've kept inside themselves.

ACTION 4. ASK THEIR OPINIONS FOR BEST SOLUTIONS AND SEEK A WIN-WIN RESOLUTION

When sufficient rapport has been established in the previous steps, and customers see that you're genuinely trying to help them, most of them will want to be fair in their negotiation with you. They'll often even lower their demands when you ask for their opinions for best solutions.

Be warned, though, that if people are still strong in their objections or show reluctance in going forward in transacting the sale, it's usually because you haven't completed some previous steps of the CLIENT-Focused Sales System. Since you don't complete every sale, you can get to this point and realize that the person just isn't going to buy. Or they want more time to make a decision. So you can ask some questions to find out where they really are.

- "What do you want to do at this point?"
- "Do you want more time to think about this?"
- "What more information can I get for you at this time?"

Argue Their Case for Them

It's been written that Abraham Lincoln as a lawyer never lost a case. He had this down-to-earth, homespun manner about him that seemed to draw juries to him, wanting to see things his way, because of his "fairness."

In his opening and closing arguments, he'd spend much of his time, at first, arguing his opponent's case. He'd mention all the good points of the other lawyer's case, conceding that there were some good points to it. He'd then tell what strong points his adversary would later bring up. Finally, he'd transition to his own points and position himself as one with the jury by saying, in essence, "While my opponent's points are good, there are more weighty matters that *we* should consider before making a decision."

He then presented his own case, explaining how the evidence overwhelmingly favored his clients' innocence.

When you sincerely understand your customers' quandary and aren't saying something to control or manipulate them into making a decision, the following statement will help you argue their cases for them. I call these the five magic words: "I understand how you feel."

After this opening statement, tell them *how* you understand. *Why* they have a right to feel the way they do. And how if you were in their situation, you might feel the same way.

When you sincerely communicate this to your clients, you keep rapport with them. The worst thing you can do is to disagree with them—even when you know their thinking is wrong or their facts a bit skewed.

Agree with Clients as Much as You Can

Look for specific points that your customers make with which you can agree. Each time you do this you build small increments of rapport. Since so much of what drives their decisions and actions comes from their emotions, the rapport you have with them may even outweigh their conscious logic.

Always remember that human beings are mostly driven by emotional feelings rather than by logic—especially at decision points.

Stay Focused on the Solutions, Not the Problems

You'll occasionally encounter risk-averse people who would rather stay focused on the problem or perceived risk than seek a solution.

Maybe, at the moment of truth, they suddenly see the risk ballooning up and overshadowing the rewards of the purchase.

When you reach this stage with someone, you might ask, "You said before that you really want to [mention a problem they wanted to solve or a solution they wanted to make happen]. How important is this to you now?"

Some people who are reluctant to make decisions may make you think they're going to buy, but later come back with more objections or want to renegotiate the price that's already been agreed on.

So you often have to go back and pick things up at the point in the CLIENT steps where things stalled out.

Reactions You Might Get from Different Personality Patterns

Up to this point, the discussions have mainly focused on the possible rewards that people might enjoy if they move forward with a purchase. Ultimately, as decision time draws near, the focus involves taking risks and making purchase commitments. It helps to understand how people with different Personality Patterns look at and respond to risks.

- *Socializers* generally avoid risks as possible ways to keep from losing other people's favor. Since their greatest need is social approval, their greatest fear is the loss of it. They often need the help and support of other people at decision time—getting opinions from friends or family. You may want to find out who they might lean on for support and involve them in the ILLUSTRATE and EVALUATE Steps.

- *Achievers* love to make decisions. They also enjoy taking calculated risks when convinced that the rewards will justify them. They aren't influenced by what others think or worried about losing favor with people. When they're convinced that the purchase will give them the bottom-line results they want, they'll make quick decisions. They are often ego-driven; when they see how their purchase will cause them to gain power or influence, they'll be strongly motivated to buy.

- *Conformers* are usually very risk-averse. They'll need to spend more time thinking about the purchase and will not make quick decisions. Any pressure you put on them will cause them to be more indecisive, freeze up, and not buy. Get them sharing with you the risks they might run by making the purchase, and listen to them. As you listen, understand, and let them know how they have a right to feel the way they do, you may help them feel comfortable enough to make a decision. They'll usually only make decisions that adhere closely to their previous purchases. They don't step very far outside their previous comfort zones.

- *Controllers* can be slow in making decisions until they feel they have all the facts and everything is in a logical order. They want to know how everything fits into their thinking and structure, how their decision helps create efficiency, safe return on investment, and good management. When they're stuck in making decisions they probably need more data, proof, or insurance from risks.

NEGOTIATE Self-Assessment

Please read each statement and ask yourself, "How descriptive is this statement of my actual behaviors with clients?" If it's always descriptive, circle 10; if it's never descriptive, circle 1; if it's sometimes descriptive, circle the appropriate number in between.

1. I always make sure I've completed the first four steps of the CLIENT-Focused Sales System before allowing myself to get into a negotiation posture.

    1 2 3 4 5 6 7 8 9 10

2. At this point of a sale I always openly welcome the concerns, questions, or objections people might have.

    1 2 3 4 5 6 7 8 9 10

3. I always keep my mind and body language open when people express negative responses.

    1 2 3 4 5 6 7 8 9 10

4. I never become defensive, argumentative, or confrontational during negotiations.

    1 2 3 4 5 6 7 8 9 10

5. I am very good at listening to what people say and paraphrasing back to them my understanding.

    1 2 3 4 5 6 7 8 9 10

    Total: _____

As you review these five statements, which one are you good at, and which one might you most like to strengthen?

Coaching Yourself on the NEGOTIATE Step

To help you understand when you've completed this step, you might want to make sure you've completed these suggestions:

1. You understand customers' concerns, objections, or questions.
2. They believe that you genuinely want to help them.
3. You've worked through their concerns.
4. They have no more concerns or questions.

When you've either made or lost a sale, come back and see if you achieved these four points. This way you'll learn from both the times you made a sale and the times you lost one.

How to Benefit the Most from This Chapter

Remember, improvement doesn't come by just reading and understanding the contents of this book, but rather by picking out one or two specific actions in each chapter that would help you and then applying them in your contacts with customers. Here are some actions you can take to benefit from what you read:

1. Continue to apply all of the CLIENT-Focused Sales System steps as they become appropriate in your daily selling.

2. Especially focus on the NEGOTIATE Step this week. Apply the concepts and actions each time you have an opportunity.
3. Identify the Personality Patterns of each person you contact, and analyze how your own patterns might connect, or disconnect with each person.
4. Fill in the NEGOTIATE Self-Assessment, and pick out one or two of the statements to strengthen.
5. Meet with your study group this week and share each other's successes and how each of you is applying the CLIENT-Focused Sales System.

How to Transition to the TRANSACT Step

When you've completed the actions for the NEGOTIATE Step, and have worked through all of the clients' concerns, it's time to go to the TRANSACT Step. Usually, before you go to this step you already know that clients are going to make a purchase decision. This step is not a "selling" one; rather it's when you already know that clients want to complete the purchase and simply want to know the details of payment, shipment, or billing.

Make sure you've dealt with all their concerns and they're ready to buy. Go to the TRANSACT Step and find out what actions or details they want to take to finalize the sale.

9

TRANSACT

EXCHANGING YOUR SOLUTIONS FOR CLIENTS' PAYMENT

*People buy, when and only when the value of the
product or service is worth more to them than
the money they will exchange for it.*

—JOHN D. MURPHY

Old "closing the sale" strategies have kept more people from closing sales than anything else.

I once answered an ad for a kitchen remodeling company. The owner came out to look at my home to give me a price. I went out to show her how to get up the steps to my front door. She had a little dog in her car that was barking like crazy, apparently wanting to tear one of my legs off. She shoved the dog back in her car, slammed the door, and said, "She doesn't like people."

Gosh, I could've figured that out by myself, but I did appreciate her warning me.

She stopped in my entryway, looked around, and asked, "If we can come to terms on price, are you prepared to buy today?"

I couldn't believe what she'd asked. Then I thought she'd read one of my books on selling and was baiting me, knowing that I'd made jokes about that old used-car-salesman opening. I double-checked her eyes to see if she was serious. She was.

My response was, "Aren't you getting a little ahead of yourself?" She wasn't deterred by my question and began telling me what kind of cabinets I should have. She then told me she was an interior designer and, as she looked around my home, that she could probably help me. I immediately visualized the interior of her car that was filled with old soft drink cups, burger wrappers, magazines, brochures, and other nondescript junk (plus the dog). Picturing her making my home look like the inside of her car prevented me from hiring her to redecorate my home.

Reflecting back, if I hadn't been such a coward, and she hadn't been so much meaner looking than me, I would've shown her the door. But since I'm only six feet, two inches tall and weigh 215 pounds, I thought that since I was outclassed, discretion was the better part of valor.

Well, that is a bit of an exaggeration, but her statements are true.

Oh, in case you're wondering, I did survive that experience. Yeah, I know, if I hadn't been such a coward I would've told her where her dog probably acquired its nastiness.

A True Transformation

Many changes have happened in the way people sell in the last couple of decades, although many salespeople are hanging on to old persuasion-focused, manipulative, adversarial, negotiation-based selling strategies.

If we go back enough years, most so-called sales training was based on *how to close sales*. *Secrets of Closing Sales* became a popular title. All kinds of gimmicks were touted that, when practiced, would help salespeople win over customers: phrases like, "A, B, C—Always be closing." "Closing is the only thing in selling." "You've got my money in your pocket, and it's my job to get it into mine."

All these old stimulus-response selling strategies clearly pitted salespeople as doing battle with customers.

Client-focused selling changes almost everything that most salespeople have been taught. I've taken it from "How can I get you to buy?" to "How can I help you enjoy the benefits you want to enjoy?" This transitions from a self focus to a client focus.

The beautiful irony is that when people buy into and begin following the instructions in this book, their sales almost immediately increase—depending, of course, on the natural sales cycle of whatever they sell.

I just had a letter from a company that implemented the information in this book a year ago and has enjoyed a 140 percent increase over the previous year. That is somewhat unusual, as typically, we see around a 25 percent overall increase with proper implementation. A president of another company called me recently and told me of an $800,000 goal they had with a specific client. But by training their people to use the Diagnostic Conflict Model found in the LISTEN Step, they ended up doing almost $1,500,000.

One major change has been in old stimulus-response selling, where the "close" was designed as a selling or convincing step. In our CLIENT-Focused Sales System, we've taken that language out, because when we've been successful in completing the first five steps, the sale has been made, and all we need to do is complete the transaction.

CLIENT-Focused Sales System

Step 6. TRANSACT: Exchanging Your Solutions for Clients' Payment

TRANSACT Actions to Practice

1. Ask what details you need to discuss at this point.
2. Listen and address each issue.
3. Review how the value exceeds the cost.
4. Ask to complete the transaction.

These actions will help you conclude a sale when the previous steps have been successfully completed. Often, though, you may think you're at the TRANSACT point, only to discover that people are not yet sold. It's here that you will want to stop and determine which steps you failed to complete, and go back and finish them if you can.

ACTION 1. ASK WHAT DETAILS YOU NEED TO DISCUSS AT THIS POINT

You've already asked this question in the previous two steps, but the real world being what it is, people don't always tell you their true feelings until they get closer to having to make a decision. If you've sold much, you know exactly what I mean.

I've shared at some length the importance of asking questions and listening to what people tell you. Not just listening—but understanding. Not just understanding what they tell you—but feeling how they feel. Not just feeling how they feel—but sincerely wanting to help them.

Most of our communication with other people takes place below the consciousness levels—between your *I Am* and your clients' *I Am*. It's not just your words that you use to communicate with others, but who you are. What your values are. What your intent is. Why you do what you do. What value you give people above the price you charge them.

In asking what details you need to understand and discuss, you'll follow this communication pattern:

1. Listen without interruption.
2. Understand what they're saying.
3. Paraphrase back to them your understanding of what they're saying.
4. Ask for clarification, making sure you fully understand them.

This process will prevent any adversarial relationships from developing and allow your clients to appreciate your understanding and desire to assist them. You'll increase your rapport and strengthen your trust.

ACTION 2. LISTEN AND ADDRESS EACH ISSUE

At this point you should have flushed out all concerns, problems, or objections in your EVALUATE and NEGOTIATE Steps. Often, though, people will bring up old issues, proving that they either need more time to make a decision or don't really want to buy and are reluctant to tell you this.

When these and other issues come up, you might ask, "How would you like to proceed at this point?" Several things can be going on in the customers' minds:

- They want what you're selling but want more time to make a decision.
- They need other people's input or support.
- They're frozen because of their fear of making a bad decision.
- They've decided to look at other options.
- Their desire for a solution wasn't as urgent as they previously expressed.

These responses can tell you that you didn't complete a previous step. You can experience several situations. You may have tried to conclude the sale so fast that you didn't even get agreement that what you recommended in the ILLUSTRATE Step was what customers really wanted, or they changed their minds and you didn't detect it.

Or you might discover that you didn't really do the EVALUATE and NEGOTIATE Steps well, even though you thought you did. Since we don't complete all the sales we attempt, sometimes we have to decide that they're just not good prospects and move on to other clients.

Again, let me encourage you to go to the Diagnostics section at the end of this book and follow the instructions for downloading the After Contact Self-Coaching Evaluation form. Checking off the points that you completed reveals the ones you didn't finish.

Don't expect perfection, but do expect excellence.

ACTION 3. REVIEW HOW THE VALUE EXCEEDS THE COST

Have you learned more of your clients' dominant buying motives at this point? Do you have new information that gives you additional insight into *why* they want to purchase your product or service? After spending more time with them, do you now understand more about their Personality Patterns and how their patterns influence their decision styles?

Remember, people buy for what the product or service will do for them or how it will make them look to others. You'll probably never know all the reasons why people decide to buy or not to buy. Many of your customers' buying motives are emotionally driven, and often they don't know either. But being observant will help you increase your ability to determine their inner, often illogical motivations.

How do the benefits of your products or services outweigh the cost to your customers? Can you be more specific about explaining them in terms that fit your clients' wishes? How can you describe these benefits in amounts, weights, measurements, dollars, time, recognition from others, or other extra value? How can you help clients visualize the specific rewards they want to enjoy?

ACTION 4. ASK TO COMPLETE THE TRANSACTION

By the time you've completed the CONNECT through NEGOTI-ATE Steps, you usually know whether your clients are ready to buy . . . or not. But if they haven't specifically vocalized a commitment, you might ask the following question: "What do we need to do to finalize this transaction?" You may phrase this question several ways, depending on your relationship with the buyer and what you're selling. This is a logical question and includes no intended manipulation as so many old "closing" questions did in the past.

Your customer's answer will reveal whether you've completed all the previous steps in the system successfully. Hopefully, you'll discover what action needs to be taken to complete the transaction. Is it a contract that needs to be signed, or obtaining a credit card number, a check, cash, or other payment options?

TRANSACT Self-Assessment

Please read each statement and ask yourself, "How descriptive is this statement of my actual behaviors with clients?" If it's always descriptive, circle 10; if it's never descriptive, circle 1; if it's sometimes descriptive, circle the appropriate number in between.

1. Before I expect to complete a transaction, I always ask if there are any other issues that need to be discussed before completing it.

    1 2 3 4 5 6 7 8 9 10

2. At this point I always want to know customers' exact thinking, even if it might be negative.

    1 2 3 4 5 6 7 8 9 10

3. I always make sure that customers believe the value they'll receive exceeds their cost.

    1 2 3 4 5 6 7 8 9 10

4. I always see this step as a win-win for both my customers and myself.

    1 2 3 4 5 6 7 8 9 10

5. I never feel any fear of rejection or reluctance to ask for a decision at this point of the sale.

    1 2 3 4 5 6 7 8 9 10

    Total: _____

Coaching Yourself on the TRANSACT Step

Here's how to know when you've completed the TRANSACT Step:

1. Everyone's concerns have been successfully worked through.
2. They understand how the benefits of your products or services will exceed their cost.
3. They want what you have.
4. You complete the appropriate purchase action.

After completing the transaction, reassure your clients that they've made a good decision. If time permits, get them talking again about how they'll enjoy the benefits of their purchase.

Practicing the CLIENT-Focused Sales System Is Self-Rewarding

When you've understood, practiced, valued, and applied the CLIENT-Focused Sales System, it will touch all three of your levels of consciousness—your *Head*, *Heart*, and *Soul*. Here's how:

1. *Head*—you'll intellectually learn the CLIENT-Focused Sales System's actions, how to carry them out, and other information about application, theory, and Personality Patterns of customers.
2. *Heart*—you'll elicit feelings and emotional responses as you practice the system. Elation, rejection, disappointment, enthusiasm, and a host of different kinds of positive

emotions emerge within you. You're now more able to handle the emotional ups and downs of selling.

3. *Soul*—you'll feed and nourish your spiritual part by your sincere acts of service. "It is more blessed to give than to receive" is a true spiritual law. Then, when you graciously receive compensation for the acts of service you've rendered, you'll also feed your inner sense of worthiness.

We see transformations all the time in our courses as people begin to practice the system. Most salespeople are trained to start from a transaction or product focus; gradual practice of the CLIENT-Focused Sales System begins working down from the *Head* to the *Heart* to the *Soul*. As you intellectually learn about the system and begin applying it, clients feel good about your purpose of creating the most value for them. When customers feel good about your sincere practice of the system, they'll be impelled to return value to you.

Your confidence grows. Fear of rejection diminishes. Result-producing activities increase. You're more energized. Your area-of-the-possible expands. Your inner sense of meaning spreads out like a healthy vine that sends down roots into soils of integrity and spiritual nourishment.

As all these dynamics occur and come into a harmonious confluence, a powerful synergy begins to develop. Your actual performance levels become significantly larger than the sum of your actual abilities.

Think about this.

Reward Yourself

Always, always reward yourself after completing a transaction. No matter how large or small. Give yourself something that you wouldn't ordinarily purchase. That's the secret—present yourself with a gift that you'd *selfishly* like to have but under normal logical, rational circumstances wouldn't go out and buy. It doesn't make a lot of difference what the cost is. Allow the size of the sale to determine that.

It's the repeated act of rewarding yourself that builds your inner motivational powers—nourishing your deep sense of worthiness. Keep your promised reward in mind when you're going through the sales steps, visualizing yourself enjoying it when you complete the transaction. Allow this to motivate you during the sales process, especially when difficulties or roadblocks come up.

After all this mental prompting, when you do complete the transaction, keep your promise and immediately go get the reward. This actual reinforcement of your success builds your confidence more than the gift you give yourself. It's a psychological enabling power. It gives you self-confidence and motivates you to think, plan, and act bigger.

Please don't underestimate the power of this reinforcing act. Promise yourself a specific reward. Allow it to drive your activities. Immediately give it to yourself after the transaction is completed. Do this over and over, and it will increase your sense of worthiness as well as your motivational effectiveness in your unconscious *I Am*.

Lagniappe

Lagniappe is an interesting word—meaning "something extra." It reminds us to always take time, when completing a sale, to give our clients something they aren't expecting. It's the mint at the end of a nice meal. Unexpected flowers after a sale. An extra service. Dropping off a new book you think a client might enjoy. Calling to pick up your customer's automobile a month after the purchase and taking it to be washed.

The secret is that it must be unexpected, not previously promised or thrown in just to close a sale. The size doesn't count, it's the surprise that makes the impact.

I once bought a car from a salesperson who, even after the sale was complete, would call me and say, "It's probably time for your service. If it's convenient today or tomorrow, I'll drop a loaner off for you and pick up your car, and I will have it back to you late in the afternoon."

Earlier I mentioned Larry Merritt, who went into the *Guinness Book of World Records* as having sold more new cars over a twenty-year period than anyone else. Within a few days after buying a car, his customers received a beautiful floral arrangement.

Early in my career and at the end of his, I met a legend in the life insurance business—Elmer Leterman. In the years of the Great Depression in 1930, when men were begging for jobs that paid $1 a day, he sold $67 million for John Hancock alone. One year in the 1930s he sold $250 million of group insurance. One of his clients was publicly quoted as saying about Elmer, "When other salespeople call on me, I catch myself saying, 'I wonder what they want,' but when Elmer comes around, I find myself saying, 'I wonder what he's bringing me this time.'"

But let me warn you of a great secret here. Give with no expectation of payback. The Roman philosopher Seneca wrote, "There is no grace in a benefit that sticks to the fingers." Release your need to receive rewards from the gifts you give. These will come by their own power, and the spiritual sweetness that comes from your giving is somewhat dulled by any attempt to manipulate positive responses back to yourself.

"He is great who confers the most benefits," wrote Emerson.

Checking In on Your Purpose

Your purpose of creating the most value for the most people nourishes your *Soul* and answers your need for meaning. As this happens at a deep, profound level, a new and more powerful motivation begins to drive you.

To develop this new spiritual energy that nourishes your *Soul*:

1. Find out how the end users of your products or services have benefited from them. If it's the person to whom you sold your solutions or the customers they sold them to, identify them and understand the rewards they enjoyed.
2. Relish these and be thankful for them, as this deepens the good that you are doing because of the people who are enjoying their lives more because of you.

The more people you touch with whatever you sell, and the more benefits it brings to more people, the natural law of reciprocity ultimately creates more blessings that come back to you.

In his insightful essay "Compensation," Emerson wrote:

Every act rewards itself, or in other words integrates itself in a twofold manner; first in the thing, or in real nature; and second in the circumstances or in apparent nature. . . . Give and it shall be given you. He that watereth shall himself be watered.

Try to calculate how many people are ultimately touched by your solution. How will it help them? What do they enjoy that they wouldn't have otherwise enjoyed? Do the benefits of your solutions extend into the second and third levels of people, beyond the person you sold to directly? Do the proud owners of the homes you sell extend their joy into their children, grandchildren, friends, and neighbors and create rich family and social memories?

Breathe in the blessings that you've helped all these people enjoy. Inhale the joy of knowing that you've created this extra value for this many people. How have their lives been made better? Healthier? More meaningful? Richer?

Allow yourself to participate in the good that you help create as a salesperson.

How to Benefit the Most from This Chapter

You may or may not have a chance to apply this step this week; hopefully you will, as this indicates that you completed sales.

Follow these suggestions and you'll have a great week:

1. Review the chapter and underline points you want to remember or practice.
2. Refer to the card or electronic device on which you wrote the six-step CLIENT-Focused Sales System and actions.
   a. Score yourself on how well you practiced the actions this week.
   b. Determine what actions you should have practiced.
   c. Identify where you are with different clients you talked to this week.
3. Reflect on your interactions with people this past week and how you communicated with different Personality Patterns.
4. Meet with your success group, with each of you sharing examples of your personal experiences this past week.

There's More to Selling Success
Than Knowing the Sales System

Different people tend to get different results from practicing the CLIENT-Focused Sales System. This raises the question: "Why?"

You'll recall I mentioned that selling success is 15 percent product and systems knowledge and 85 percent attitudes, emotional factors, values, and inner belief boundaries. The next three chapters will deal with these issues. Specifically, we'll think about:

- Deeper drivers of your sales success.
- Handling your emotional ups and downs.
- Turning negative, pessimistic thoughts into positive, optimistic ones.
- Releasing spiritual and emotional toxins.

The last six chapters have dealt with the *Head*, or knowing how to practice the CLIENT-Focused Sales System; the rest of the book is about your *Heart* and *Soul*—the 85 percent that influences your actual sales.

PART III

DEEPER DRIVERS OF SALES EFFECTIVENESS

The whole drift of my education goes to persuade me
that the world of our present consciousness is only one
out of many worlds of consciousness that exist.

—WILLIAM JAMES

10

PERSIST

WORKING THROUGH YOUR EMOTIONAL UPS AND DOWNS

Never give up!—if adversity presses,
Providence wisely has mingled the cup,
And the best counsel, in all your distresses,
Is the stout watchword of "Never give up!"

—MARTIN FARQUHAR TUPPER

Never give up! Easy to say. Harder to do!

But if you're following your purpose, doing what gives you a sense of meaning, you can almost always find a way to work through the natural challenges that will certainly confront you. I've never forgotten the advice of a very wise man who told me, "You'll be just as successful as the size of problems you take responsibility for solving, and then solve."

Think I'm being too preachy? Please read my story, and see if you think I've earned the right to give you this advice. I've experienced many problems, many of which seemed insurmountable, but they all steered me into totally different directions that proved to be much better than the courses I was on.

One of the first of many business reversals came when I was a junior in college. I'd paid my way through the first two years by making and selling hand-tooled leather belts and doing construction work in the summers. I always seemed to have money.

Students showed up from California the third year wearing Levis without belts. This quickly became the rage. And . . . almost overnight I was out of business. I couldn't give belts away after that.

Six of us lived in a garage apartment, each paying $10 per month toward the rent. In a West Texas town with three colleges and so many kids hunting jobs, I couldn't find one anywhere. After paying my tuition and buying books, I had almost no money left. The college had a farm and a dairy, and a friend worked there and gave me gallons of milk. I lived one whole semester on saltine crackers crumbled up in cold milk.

The second semester I got a job in afternoons and on weekends in a supermarket unloading trucks, stocking shelves, and mopping floors. I earned 65 cents per hour and was thrilled to have the job. I got to learn from one of the best leaders I've ever met. Joe Jordan was the manager of the store, and I'd never seen anyone who could build up people like he could. Years later, the coaching and leadership courses I've written have mostly been patterned after the working model I saw in Joe.

Looking back, it's impossible to calculate exactly how much I did earn the next few decades, because of what I learned from Joe Jordan.

Had I not needed to take the 65-cents-an-hour job, I wouldn't have met Joe, and I couldn't have written the coaching and leadership courses I've done.

When I was twenty-six years old, I borrowed all the money I could, with no experience whatsoever, and opened a contemporary furniture and interior design business—Furniture Fashions, Inc. We had a Strategic Air Command base in our city, and half of our sales were to their personnel. Five years after I started the business, the government announced the closure of the base. Our sales were immediately cut in half. I began to lose money but stayed in denial, thinking I could pull out. I didn't know what to do, as I'd planned to stay in that business for the rest of my life.

Blessing of Defeat

A friend, Joe Barnett, told me I should go into training. I knew nothing about it, but I didn't know much about anything else either, so I put together a leadership program and conducted it at a church, with great results. I committed to conducting courses at churches for no pay for a year, just to get a reputation. To have money to live on, I liquidated the store. After paying all my bills and leasing out my building, I had less than $1,000 left to support my wife, two children, house payment, two car payments, and so on.

I have no idea how we made it, but we did. That year we got two income tax refunds we hadn't applied for. Other things began to happen—all at the very last minute when we had no food in our house and bills to pay.

There's much more to the story. I saw lives change each evening in the courses I was conducting. Now, forty-eight years later, more than 1.5 million people have gone through our courses in 130 nations. We have trained more than 30,000 facilitators to conduct these courses in all kinds of companies and organizations.

What a blessing it was to have the store go broke.

Another Growth Experience

In 1980 a client went broke, owing me $600,000. It gutted me. I had to let fifteen employees go, pinch, squeeze, and sell everything I could. I was broke; I owed a bank $200,000, and I owed printers and the IRS other amounts. Not knowing what I was going to do to survive financially, I was at a speakers' conference in Chicago, and out of nowhere a man offered to set up one-day seminars for me to conduct.

The man who owed us the money had owned a chain of car dealerships. He was a very honest man, and when interest rates went to 21 percent, he went broke. As I share with you in another chapter of this book, this indirectly helped me make a large sale to Chevrolet seven years later that dwarfed the loss.

What a blessing it was to lose $600,000, and be broke for a while.

Not Finished with Problems

Fast-forward a few years, after our business had been very successful, my partner and I decided to sell our company. We did. I had several million dollars. I started a new company and was quickly incurring losses from $60,000 to $80,000 per month. I invested in some real estate just before the crash of 2008. One piece was a home that I thought I could resell for a $1 million profit. I paid $2.8 million for it, had to sell it later, and lost $1.6 million on it. And there was other stuff. All of a sudden I had lost almost everything. As property values dropped around 50 percent, I didn't have the income I'd had for years, and I couldn't keep servicing the debt. I lost around $6 million.

My last property was a second home in Santa Fe, New Mexico,

which I bought in 2004 for $1,325,000, taking a mortgage of just under $800,000 and paying cash for the balance. In 2009–2010, things began to go downhill fast. Not having the income to service the debt, I began to borrow on the home in Santa Fe. $225,000 at one bank. $100,000 at another. The IRS suddenly disallowed some write-offs and wanted $102,000 more from me. The State of Arizona followed, wanting another $39,000. City taxes in Santa Fe of $12,000; back homeowner's fee of $10,000.

Pretty soon these tend to add up to real money.

I listed the Santa Fe home for $1,395,000. No offers for months. Finally got one for $895,000. Wouldn't work. More months went by. Creditors became very aggressive, giving me deadlines. I stalled them as long as I could. But the day of reckoning was clearly at hand. Everyone began to file liens on the property. Still no workable offers.

What Is the Worst That Can Happen?

After working through denial, anger, guilt, depression, anxiety, and dread, I asked myself, "What is the worst that can happen if all this falls apart?" "How will I handle it if things do crash?" That took some sober introspection and meditation.

To emotionally deal with all of it, I had to change how I defined who I am. I began to say to myself, "I define myself by who I *am*, not what I *possess*. I'm still the same person as before. Actually I know more now than ever before."

Some difficult, foggy days followed that. Unbelievable stress.

One day, when I was literally ten days away from foreclosure by the banks, the IRS, and the state, a lady walked into the house, looked around, and said to her real estate agent, "I want this home."

She was a cash buyer, no mortgage. When she found out how much was owed on the property, she offered to pay everything off and give me $10,000 above that. We called the lienholders, telling them of the situation, and within three weeks everything was closed and paid off. Otherwise, I would've had to file for bankruptcy.

Did all of that happen the way it did by pure chance? I don't think so. Did it happen for a purpose? I believe it did.

What a blessing to get to start over again.

Forced to Look at Myself and Learn

What did I learn from all of this? Well, a bunch of things. How *stupid* I was to get into that position. *Proud* of friends who supported me. *Embarrassment* that I had to trim 85 percent out of my previous monthly living expenses—which I did. *Realization* that I couldn't fly first class to London or Paris anytime I wanted to do so. Some *depression* and *anxiety* over how I'd get out of the mess I was in. *Gratitude* that I still have the knowledge and experience to write materials that help people enjoy higher qualities of life. *Searching* for what I'm supposed to learn from all this. *Enthusiasm* over how this bad series of events will turn out to be a blessing for me. *Confirmation* that with the Lord's help I can handle some pretty difficult challenges and keep going.

Mainly, I learned that *things*—Mercedes, BMWs, Porsches, multimillion-dollar homes—don't define me. It's *who* I am and *why* I'm on this planet now that defines me. It was difficult to admit that my pride and ego drove much of my past actions—describing myself as the "founder of," the "author of," "the owner of . . ."

A New Business

So at age eighty I'm experiencing the exhilaration of starting a new business. It's taken all my life experiences to enable me to write a world-class new course—The Authentic Salesperson. It truly changes people's lives and helps them enjoy higher levels of career and life success. One year after our first three pilots, one major company incresed its sales 140 percent, another doubled its sales, and another almost tripled its sales over the previous year.

This book had to be preceded by some devastating moments, or my message wouldn't have the authenticity that you deserve. Otherwise my advice would be hollow indeed. Besides all that, if all of these things hadn't happened and I hadn't written this book, I would have never met you.

But mainly, I needed to have earned the right to make the following statement: *I have learned that no matter the size of the problem, if we persist and are willing to go to the wall, trying everything we can think of to solve it, in the Scheme of Things, at the very last minute things work out. Solutions suddenly show up. We passed the test.*

We make our own choices. When we want increased life benefits, we must understand that we have to grow to get there. Growing takes the form of life challenges that test us, strengthen us, and prepare us to handle higher levels of growth.

I believe that there's a Natural Law that says, "Prove to me that you won't give up, no matter what may come, and then I'll send you a solution."

It helps to take the following steps:

1. Identify what's the worst that could happen, and decide you can handle it if it comes to that.

2. Believe that every adversity brings with it an equivalent or greater benefit.

Every problem I've had in my life has ushered in better things or new opportunities into my life. I believe this will continue as long as I live.

Persistence wins over talent. It learns from life's natural rough spots. It carries you through challenges that are just tough enough to make you want to run for cover. It delivers growth, maturity, and wisdom for us to carry into our futures.

Allow me to share with you another fact of life.

Life Is Difficult

"Life is difficult," wrote Scott Peck in the opening of his excellent book *The Road Less Traveled*.

This is a great truth, one of the greatest truths. It is a great truth because once we truly see this truth, we transcend it. Once we truly know that life is difficult—once we truly understand and accept it—then life is no longer difficult. Because once it is accepted, the fact that life is difficult no longer matters.

Persistence, like its first-cousin discipline, is driven by much deeper forces than just knowledge. Most of our persistence problems involve emotions more than knowledge. We hear statements like these all the time: "I know I shouldn't eat ice cream when I'm on a diet." "I know I should make more calls for appointments, but I'm emotionally hand-cuffed by debilitating fear of rejection." "Every time I finish one month, I begin to worry about the next one."

Few jobs or careers present the emotional challenges of selling. Our successes are mixed with uncertainties, lost sales, occasional difficult people, and the ever-present press for production. It's enough to cause us to look for safe jobs like javelin catchers, porcupine sorters, or traffic directors in the center of intersections in Mexico City.

Okay, so life is difficult. Accepting this, dealing with it, and succeeding despite it is what makes life interesting. It's the price we pay for the benefits we receive. It goes with the territory. Success isn't free, nor should it be.

What is it in people that helps us survive and succeed when times get tough? We may call it discipline, willpower, or tenacity, but how do we develop these not-so-common traits? Are we born with them? Are they developed more in the good or bad times of our lives?

The tensile strength of iron is developed by extreme heat. So is the tensile strength of people.

Accept the Fact That Selling Can Be Difficult at Times

The selling profession offers many opportunities and benefits. It also presents frequent challenges. We must measure the two against each other and decide whether this is the career for us.

A baseball hitter is thrilled to strike out seven out of ten times. He'll earn in a week what it may take us a year or more to earn. A quarterback can earn a high income while not completing all of his passes. In both of these cases, the athletes have accepted the failure-to-success ratios as realities of their professions. They just hunker down and stay steady in the saddle, knowing that their efforts will average out.

So must you as a salesperson.

Selling gets easier—releasing much of the fear of rejection, discipline, and the unknown future—as you internalize the following definitions of success and failure that I first mentioned in Chapter 1.

A Prosperity Balance

When you internalize the following two points in your *Head, Heart,* and *Soul,* your whole view of selling, view of your abilities, values, sense of worthiness, and belief in the efficacy of your solutions will take a dramatic change. You'll almost immediately look into the mirror and see a new person.

1. Success in selling is seeing as many people as you can to see who wants or needs your help. If they want or need your help, you help them. If they neither want nor need your help, you haven't failed; you've succeeded in finding out whom you can help.
2. Failure is finding people who want or need your help, but you won't help them. It's also failing to contact people who might need your help because you're afraid you can't relate to them, or they might think you're just trying to earn money off them.

Simply changing the definition from *selling* to *helping* softens the potential emotional challenges of your job. I've seen many people become transformed when accepting this new definition of selling. When you deeply believe that your role is to see as many people as you can to see who you can help, and if they want or need it, you help them—you are freed of truckloads of emotional garbage. Fear of rejection virtually evaporates.

Should people not want or need your help, you haven't failed, you've succeeded in finding out who you can help. This is okay, as not everyone will need your help.

When you truly see your role as helping people who want or need your help, you'll feel your fears of rejection, or other negative emotional responses common to selling, slowly vanish.

Increasing Your Prosperity Consciousness

Prosperity consciousness is looking into the future and seeing predominately good things ahead. It's the *Head, Heart,* and *Soul* all believing that over the long term, everything will turn out well. It's believing that all life circumstances can be learning experiences. Problems can help you grow. Good will prevail. There is hope for a greater tomorrow.

It's visiting the future you want to happen, then returning to the present, and planning for what you saw.

While a prosperity consciousness is the effect of certain beliefs and thinking, we can develop it by actively creating more and greater value than people pay us. Focusing on this overage that our clients receive helps us build a prosperity consciousness. It's also essential that we believe we should be compensated consistently with the value we help create—recognizing that there are many kinds of compensation.

I am thrilled to receive letters from our course participants and readers of my books telling me of the increases in their sales and income because of practicing the success principles. Almost all of their increased income far exceeds the tuition they paid to take my course.

J. W. Rayhons, one of our local facilitators, recently told me about seeing a person who had been in one of our courses about three years ago on an airplane. Ironically, they were both seated in aisle seats across from each other.

The course participant worked for a bank and supervised three branches. One of our sessions is a detailed goal-setting and achievement process in which participants write down goals for different areas of their lives. Then they write out action plans and define the rewards of reaching the goals. She mentioned to her group that she'd like to set a goal of getting the vice president's job, but she was afraid that she wasn't qualified for it.

Her group persuaded her to go ahead and set a goal for that job, and she did. Long story short, she got the job. That was around three years ago. The bank was bought out, and now she oversees three states and 110 branches.

Of course, I have no idea how much her income has increased, but I'm sure it would be in the tens of thousands. I do know that I cleared $300 on the tuition of the course after costs. How do I feel about that exchange?

Very good.

With these thoughts in mind, please take a couple moments and score yourself on the following self-assessment.

Persistence Self-Assessment

Please read each statement and ask yourself, "How descriptive is this statement of my actual sales behaviors?" If it's always descriptive, circle 10; if it is never descriptive, circle 1; if it's sometimes descriptive, circle the appropriate number in between.

1. I have a history of strong resilience and working through struggles.

    1   2   3   4   5   6   7   8   9   10

2. I take complete ownership of my problems and emotional feelings.

    1 2 3 4 5 6 7 8 9 10

3. I am not deterred on my job by rejection, discouragement, or seeming defeats.

    1 2 3 4 5 6 7 8 9 10

4. I immediately replace fears of rejection by reviewing the benefits I might help customers enjoy.

    1 2 3 4 5 6 7 8 9 10

5. I never let people down who love, respect, and have faith in me.

    1 2 3 4 5 6 7 8 9 10

6. I have strong people from whom I draw support when I'm engulfed with fears or frustrations.

    1 2 3 4 5 6 7 8 9 10

7. I keep an even emotional tone through all kinds of experiences.

    1 2 3 4 5 6 7 8 9 10

8. I may not like to do certain activities, but I do them anyway.

    1 2 3 4 5 6 7 8 9 10

9. I've found that when I do activities I fear to do, my fear soon diminishes.

    1 2 3 4 5 6 7 8 9 10

10. I always believe that success is just around the corner.

1 2 3 4 5 6 7 8 9 10

Total: _____

What did you learn? On which statement did you score yourself highest? Lowest? Realizing that none of us is perfect, what actions might you take to increase both?

Now I'll guide you through a series of actions you can take to develop stronger persistence. You'll deal with some of the natural emotions that stop or slow down many salespeople.

Set Motivational Rewards for Performing Dreaded Activities

Look at your history of persistence, and you can break it up into specific incidents where you chose to do or not to do difficult activities. There can be many reasons why you made the choices you did. Probably 85 percent of them were emotionally driven. Logic had little to do with many of your decisions to act, as your *I Know* knew very well what you *should* do.

Over a period of time you form certain behavior patterns. They become comfortable. So you continue doing them until your habits, expectations, and areas-of-the-possible are slowly cemented into a rock-hard emotional mass. From then on you unconsciously repeat these old, accepted patterns, never questioning their authenticity. Continual yielding patterns, like call reluctance, soon weaken us and make it easier to put dreaded things off or just quit doing them altogether.

Let me share with you a self-motivation process I learned and began doing several years ago. Whenever I found myself getting lazy, not wanting to call on certain people, or not believing I could sell on certain levels, I'd write down the activities that I didn't want to do. Then I'd promise myself a reward when I did something I was avoiding.

The rewards don't have to be spectacular things. They can be things like:

- A special dinner with your spouse or friend.
- A round of golf.
- Going home, flopping in your easy chair, and vegging out after a tough week.
- A massage, pedicure, or manicure.
- A new pair of shoes.
- Serving lunch at a homeless shelter.

When you identify an activity that you don't want to do or that is outside your comfort zone:

1. Write it out and keep it handy.
2. List the reward you'll give yourself when you do the dreaded activity.
3. Read it several times each day, visualizing the enjoyment of the reward.

Over time this process will help you build stronger habits of doing the needed result-producing activities that'll take you to higher production levels.

You'll also be amazed at the personal growth this process will help you develop—stretching into several areas of your life.

But you must be true to yourself and pay yourself when you perform the activity. Don't withhold the reward.

Breaking Yielding Patterns

Most of us have developed behavior patterns that operate automatically. When we encounter certain situations, our inner emotional guidance systems either crank up the fear or lower it. We stand and fight, or we run away. Meeting a proverbial bear on a trail, our natural response is to break and run. The "bear on a trail" for salespeople can be what lies behind the client's door that we're afraid we might not be able to handle. Or the bear could be the fourth lost sale this past week, causing us to want to move to a safer place like a war zone in Beirut.

We all have developed certain behavioral patterns growing up. Our parents, teachers, coaches, perceived successes or defeats, and genetics have all influenced us. I was ridiculed, criticized, and beaten down as a child and teenager. This caused me to have a low opinion of myself and a high degree of pent-up anger, which caused me to mishandle it by being highly critical of others.

Before I felt comfortable with others, I needed to know I'd get their acceptance and not rejection or criticism. Because I badly needed people's acceptance and disliked conflict with people, I developed yielding patterns—actions I should perform, but would rather not, so I put them off. Do you exhibit any yielding patterns? When you encounter necessary but dreaded activities, do you find a less threatening activity to complete instead? Wait until next week? Kill some time so you won't have to do that today? Procrastinate?

These automatic emotional responses operate quite apart from our conscious, logical minds. Any habit can be changed by substituting positive actions or self-talk. But first, we need to identify ingrained responses we want to change, and decide that we don't want them hanging around and messing up our lives. Then, we can select positive, action-oriented statements to replace the yielding ones that have been planted in our *I Am* dimensions.

Years ago, after learning a bit about mind conditioning, I began to understand that avoidant behaviors weren't getting me anywhere. I wrote this statement on an index card: *I enjoy calling on people, and people enjoy my calling on them.* I began saying it to myself both silently and out loud when I could. I said it hundreds of times, until the day came that my emotional responses began to change. I began to enjoy calling on people, rather than dreading it.

The Programming in My *I Am* Had Changed

Think of a behavior, belief, or attitude that you'd like to change. Grab something to write on, or your electronic device, and enter a statement that describes how you'd like to feel, act, or think in that situation. For example should your desire be to contact people of higher net worth, you might craft a self-suggestion: "I can create higher value for people by contacting people with higher needs for my help."

Then do as I've done many times: Repeat it to yourself over and over until you begin to form an inner belief that motivates you to take the action you were afraid to do before.

An old friend, Jack Fuqua, began to say to himself, "I do the thing I fear to do," as he was building his life insurance business. After programming this belief into his *I Am*, he gathered up the courage to call on one of the wealthiest men in his city. As it turned out, other advisors were afraid to contact this man because of his wealth and political power. In Jack's case, the man welcomed him and was open to help. He bought a substantial insurance policy from Jack.

This belief-changing process doesn't happen instantly. It takes time to erase and replace those old thinking patterns. But guess what? You've still got all your future to grow.

Having a Compelling Reason to Change

Before going through the effort of changing well-established habits or behavior patterns, you first need a compelling reason to change. *Your level of desire must exceed the discipline it takes to go through the change.* Your desire for greater confidence and less contact avoidance must exceed the amount of work and disruption that changing old habits or behavior patterns will cause. Your desire for growth must be greater than and guide your discipline to stay focused on the replacement process I just shared with you. The good news is that the bits of discipline you develop give you more confidence, which then strengthens additional discipline.

When facing situations that create emotional responses of fear, anxiety, or avoidance, you can begin to say to yourself:

> I won't allow myself to give in to this negative emotion. I owe it to myself, my family, my customers, and my organization to help as many people as possible and to be compensated according to the value I create for customers.

Here's an exercise you can do that, in time, will help change old fixed activity behaviors. These are sample statements that can become key influencers, and you can customize them with your own words. By repeating them several times daily, you'll soon plant them into your *I Am* as beliefs. When this happens, and when you need to be reminded to do them, your *I Am* will send the signal to your *I Feel,* and it will energize and influence your *I Know* to take action and do the activity.

Read through the following list of key influencers, along with the sample statements, and then design a couple that fit your current needs:

- Yourself. "I owe it to myself to earn success and self-respect in my own eyes."
- Spouse, friend, partner, or another person who loves you and wants you to succeed. "I owe it to them to provide for them on the highest level of success that I can."
- Personal stewardship. "I have been given the opportunity to help a lot of people, and I owe it to them to help as many as I can."
- Family. "I owe it to my family to provide them with the high standard of living and education they deserve."
- Special mentors. "I pay back and honor friends and mentors when I practice the principles I learned from them."
- Employers and managers. "I owe them a work ethic and job performance level that earns their highest respect."
- Organization. "It has provided me with a good position, and I owe it to the owners or stakeholders to represent them in the most confident and professional manner."
- Associates and people who look up to you. "I will be a good example of strength, persistence, and a strong work ethic to my associates."

Please design two statements that fit your unique situations, and write them on index cards or your electronic device. Say them over and over to yourself several times each day. Each time you do, visualize yourself performing the statement. This will in time inscribe these beliefs on the walls of your unconscious *I Am*, as a value or guiding belief. As this happens you'll be emotionally equipped to do the things you previously didn't want to do.

Let me emphasize that these beliefs must be implanted in your *I Am*, not just your *I Know*. In your *Heart* and *Soul*, in addition to your *Head*.

Describe Your Feelings in Writing

Here's a good way to deal with your fears, doubts, or moments when you question your wisdom for getting into selling. Paul G. Stoltz, PhD, in his book *Adversity Quotient*, gives us some good advice:

> Expressing feelings in writing creates chemical changes in your body, resulting in better health. Perhaps because it enhances one's sense of control.

According to Dr. Stoltz, we can develop stronger control over our negative responses by writing them out. Getting them out of our minds and on paper helps us understand that our fears are often not as real as we've imagined them to be. Writing them out can also drain some of the negative emotions and the influence they have over us.

Journaling, or writing out your thoughts and feelings, can have a great therapeutic benefit.

Take out a pad of paper or your electronic device and complete the following statements:

1. "The very thought of having to [describe a dreaded action] causes me to feel like [describe your feelings]."

"Rather than allowing this limitation to define me, here's how I choose to define myself: [describe your choice of self-definition]."

2. "Dealing with a difficult person like [name of difficult person] causes me to feel [describe the feelings you experience with that person]."

   "The worst that could happen to me if I contact that person is [describe the worst that could happen to you]."

3. "Being rejected when trying to get appointments with the last few people makes me want to [describe the actions you'd like to take]."

   "But if I really want to be successful, I should [describe a needed action to replace one you shouldn't take]."

4. "When getting objections from people, I tend to [describe the feelings you sometimes get]."

   "My self-esteem is strong enough that I will respond by [define your response]."

5. "When the time comes to ask for a purchase decision, I tend to [describe your emotions]."

   "But, realizing that it's not about me, but rather it's about my helping them enjoy the benefits I can give them, I'll [describe your reaction]."

These are examples you can use or change to fit your specific needs. When you write out or enter your own fears and frustrations, put a positive spin on them and you'll often see the negative power dissolve. Humor helps also. Create something funny around your fears.

Years ago when I first met Dr. Maxwell Maltz, I was intimidated by his fame, professional status, and demeanor. His book *Psycho-Cybernetics* had sold in the millions of copies, and I was just getting my training business going. On one of my first visits with him in his

New York office and residence, his wife, Anne, came into the reception room and greeted me. She commented on the day and said, "It's such a beautiful spring day that I hung Maxie's long johns outside to air out." Here we were in the middle of Manhattan, on the eighteenth-floor penthouse of an office and medical building, with the doctor's long johns flapping in the breeze on their patio above 57 West 57th Street. This made me laugh, and most of the awe I had for him went away. Humor brought him down to a human dimension.

We now know that different experiences can cause our brain functions to change, causing certain emotional reactions.

A Russian research team headed by Pjotr Garjajev discovered that living human DNA can be changed and rearranged with spoken words and phrases. Other research has shown that just thinking positive or negative thoughts can alter brain patterns. It appears that when continuous suggestions are fed to your mind, and a corresponding benefit visualized, eventually new belief patterns are developed.

You can enhance this by finding a quiet place away from distractions and conducive to a peaceful mind-set. As you repeat your written self-suggestions, immediately visualize the rewards you'll enjoy when your beliefs, attitudes, or emotions are changed into the strong ones you want them to be.

Continue doing this exercise, and within a few weeks you'll begin to notice changes in your feelings and automatic behaviors.

Accept the Worst That Can Happen in a Fear Situation

When you experience fear situations, or times when you simply don't want to expend the energy to face the tasks of the day, here's a helpful mental exercise that you can perform. Ask yourself the following question when you feel fear, worry, or anxiety keeping you from doing what you should do: "What's the worst thing that could happen to me if I call or contact this very disagreeable person?"

The rest of your interior dialogue might go like this:

Answer: "I would be rejected and maybe not make a sale."

Okay, if this happened, would you be hurt physically?

"No."

Would you still be able to eat, sleep, and drive your car?

"Uh, yes."

Would your kids completely quit loving you?

"No."

Would your whole life be wrecked?

"Probably not."

Would you be put in prison?

"No."

All right, if the worst actually happened, you wouldn't be hurt physically; you'd still be able to eat, sleep, and drive your car; you wouldn't be put into prison; your kids would still love you; and your whole life wouldn't be wrecked. Do I understand all this correctly?

"Yes, you understand me correctly."

Okay, then, what's the problem?

(A little overdramatic, but you get the point.)

Selling does present personal and relationship challenges. People who don't sell can never understand this. So to handle all the challenges, you must believe that the rewards you want to enjoy outweigh the problems that you face in reaching them, or you should get another job.

If the Worst Happens, You'll Still Be You

Usually, even if the worst happens—you get rejected, ignored, put off, or other negative responses—you'll still be you. You'll still be the same height and weight and have the same name. Your mother will still love you. The sun will still come up in the morning. None of your feared experiences will change any of these features or factors. The only hurt can be emotional, but only if you misinterpret it and allow it to have a negative impact on you.

Sometimes the nastiest of buyers can become your best customers. Or the most critical ones can become your admirers. Like Mr. Latimer, the office manager of a chemical company, who I called on my first week of selling office systems and equipment.

I'd just gotten out of college, was twenty-one years old, and was given a list of customers to call on. I went in to the counter and asked to see him. He came out of his office, looked at me with little or no emotion, and said, "Don't you think you're a little too young to be selling office equipment?" Without saying another word, he turned and walked back to his desk.

I called on him a few more times, getting similar treatment. To deal with the rejection he gave me, and to assuage the emotional wounds he'd inflicted on me, afterward I'd go to the nearest coffee shop, sit and suck my thumb, and deflect his sucker punch by meditating on how much my mother loved me. What a nice person she thought I was. If that didn't work, I'd confess some of my sins to God, hoping he'd somehow let me know that he'd just proportionally increased his love for me.

I couldn't tell whether God was listening during my missives to him from the coffee shop, because Mr. Latimer still didn't treat me with a lot of warm fuzziness. I soon quit calling on him (Mr. Latimer, not God), and started driving by the company, telling myself that I'd show him that I could be a good salesperson. I actually used that bit of self-motivation to keep me going.

Well, fast-forward thirty years. I got a call from him—out of the blue—wanting to meet with me. My first sales book, *The Best Seller*, was published in 1984 by Prentice-Hall, and he'd bought a copy. He'd forgotten me years before this, if he'd ever remembered me. In our meeting he didn't connect me with the salesperson who'd called on him years before. He now owned his own chemical company and liked my book, bought it for his salespeople, and wanted to know if I might be available to come and do some training for his people.

Waiting to see if he recognized or remembered me, I finally decided that he didn't, so I told him. We both got a laugh from the situation. He wanted me to autograph his book. I signed it by writing, "To the man most responsible for my success as an office equipment salesman."

My point? Well, if we want it to, we can even use rejections to motivate us to prove we can be successful.

Another Look at Your LifeStages

Since humans are complex bundles of motivation, there's often stuff going on in our lives that influences our activity levels. Your child is doing poorly in school. You're going through a divorce. A new competitor just moved to town. The worry, stress, pressure, and sleepless nights have worn on your sense of worthiness that resides in your *I Am*, your *Soul*. You can't focus on your work. Your issue may not be your lack of discipline in making calls or solving difficult problems that come up. It can be something totally unrelated to your work. But something is robbing you of sufficient focus and energy to do your work.

Often, these non-work-related challenges get shoved aside, but they still create drags on us. Any conflicts in your life will usually influence all parts of your life.

To help you understand more of these conflicts, let's go back and look at the Progression of LifeStages model that I showed you in Chapter 1. Review the following stages.

1. Struggling
   a. Concerns—"I'm sinking fast and about to go under."
   b. Focus—almost totally on self and how one's life can be damaged.
   c. Motivation—to keep the worst from happening.
2. Coping
   a. Concerns—"I'm afraid of what's going to happen to me, and I must find a way to keep it from occurring."
   b. Focus—on negative consequences on self and loved ones.
   c. Motivation—"fight or flight."
3. Learning
   a. Concerns—"How can I find a way out and prevent all this from happening again?"
   b. Focus—on understanding causes of problems and seek solutions.
   c. Motivation—to move past pain and ease tensions.
4. Stabilizing
   a. Concerns—"I'm seeking stability and attempting to learn from the past so as not to make the same mistakes."

     b. Focus—on reducing risks or future problems and beginning to look ahead.

     c. Motivation—to build on a solid base.

5. Succeeding

     a. Concerns—"I'm doing pretty well and am focused on expanding my knowledge, skills, and successes."

     b. Focus—outward on expanding success and creating value for others.

     c. Motivation—to increase personal and professional success, build relationships, and discover new talents and abilities.

6. Growing

     a. Concerns—"All my material needs are being filled; I want to give my life to higher purposes."

     b. Focus—outward on creating value for others and enjoying the rewards of doing so.

     c. Motivation—to mine all inner spiritual resources and become all one can become.

7. Evolving

     a. Concerns—"I want to move past physical or material values and develop deeper spiritual understandings.

     b. Focus—totally off oneself and on the betterment of humankind.

     c. Motivation—to develop greater wisdom and understanding to help solve greater problems and contribute to the knowledge bank of the universe.

Points to Remember

The following points will help you learn the most from the seven stages:

1. Whatever LifeStages you're on, you're primarily concerned with satisfying those specific needs and blinded to higher or lower stages.
2. You can be on different stages simultaneously in different areas of your life, although areas with the lowest stages will usually dominate your thinking and demand greater attention.
3. When a LifeStages is satisfied, you'll automatically move to the next higher one in that part of your life.
4. Your goals will be unconsciously screened out unless they address your present LifeStages.
5. Your goals should be focused on satisfying your current stages; which will then automatically move you to the next higher one.

Plotting Your LifeStages

For each category in the following chart, place a check mark in the appropriate column, with 1 being Struggling and 7 being Evolving:

As you plotted your stages on the chart, what did you learn? What are the two lowest stages? How might these be influencing your life and selling? Remember that these lowest stages will tend to dominate your thinking, energy, and sense of self-worth until they are satisfied.

	1	2	3	4	5	6	7
Financial							
Social							
Family							
Career							
Spiritual							
Personal Health							

Taking Actions to Satisfy Your Lowest Stages

Like most people, you may also be setting the wrong goals. The wrong goals are ones we set that don't address our actual needs in each LifeStage. The secret of personal growth and goal achievement is to take specific actions that will satisfy your lowest stages. As you satisfy one stage, you'll automatically move up to higher ones.

What specific actions might you take to satisfy the two lowest stages? Make a note to yourself, saying: "To satisfy this LifeStage in my financial life, I'll take the actions of [name the actions you will take]. When I do, I'll enjoy the benefits of [name the benefits you will enjoy]."

Here, you're listing the following points:

1. The LifeStage you're on in that part of your life.
2. The actions you'll take to move to the next higher stage.
3. The rewards you'll enjoy when you move to the next higher stage.

I like the way the great Benjamin Franklin explained this human challenge.

I decided that I wished to live without committing any fault at any time. But as I pursued this endeavor, I soon found it was a task more difficult than I had first imagined it would be. While I employed care in guarding against one fault, I was often surprised by my laxity in another.

Years later, he wrote this self-appraisal in his autobiography.

I realized that the more I developed in one area, the more room for growth I discovered in another. I also noticed that frequent were the times when I caught myself slipping back in one or more areas. The more satisfied I became with myself, the more humility I lost.

My advice is to work on one or two stages at a time, and don't get swamped by the need to achieve perfection in all areas of your life immediately.

Coordinating the Decisions in Your *I Know* with the Wisdom in Your *I Am*

In his runaway bestseller *The Road Less Traveled*, Scott Peck writes:

We have spoken of the fact that the unconscious part of our mind is the possessor of extraordinary knowledge. It knows more than we know, "we" being defined as our conscious self.

Writing about personal growth, he goes on to elaborate:

It is a process of the conscious mind coming into synchrony with the unconscious.

Translated, this means that when we make decisions with our *I Know* to act in ways that are congruent with the "spirit of truth" in our *I Am*, we align our mental, emotional, and spiritual dimensions. This synchronicity then produces an expanded inner power in our *I Feel*, generating stronger personal effectiveness.

But when we decide to act out self-focused behaviors, they interact with the spirit of truth in our *I Am*, creating a conflict that triggers negative emotions of fear, anxiety, and contact avoidance.

You haven't heard this put into a sales context, have you? This, of course, brings up the question, "What is 'truth'?" Let me list a few synonyms:

Authenticity

Veracity

Realness

Faithfulness

Steadfastness

Constancy

Loyalty

Honor

Trustworthiness

Integrity

Accuracy

Purity

Correctness

Genuineness

So what's all this got to do with successful selling? First of all, practicing all the actions of the CLIENT-Focused Sales System causes you to perform activities that are congruent with the spiritual values housed in your *I Am*. Choosing to practice them interacts with your inner spirit of truth, triggering positive emotions in your *I Feel*, which then give energy and support to the knowledge in your *I Know*.

This gives you increased confidence, courage, energy, and the will to do the activities that yield sales success.

Please stop reading for a couple of moments and carefully notice the cause and effect in the last few paragraphs.

From a self-focused standpoint, we scuffle and grab as much for ourselves as we can, ignorant to the fact that these self-focused behaviors often rob us of the joy in life that we long to have.

The following paradoxical actions are in harmony with the spirit of truth in our *I Am*. They have been hardwired into the emotional and spiritual DNA of your *Soul*. Making choices congruent with these spiritual laws trigger emotional powers, enhancing your result-producing activities, which leads to increased success.

- Do the right thing because it's the right thing to do.
- Go the extra mile and give the customer more than they expect to receive.
- Focus on understanding and creating value for people, and they'll create value for you.
- Tell the truth in all situations, unless it would hurt someone.
- Do unto others as you would want them to do unto you.
- Create high value for others and enjoy high levels of compensation and prosperity in return.

When we choose to act, perform, or respond consistently with these "truth" statements, we are rewarded with new energies, confidence, and achievement drive. Again, you've probably never heard this in any of your sales training.

Every Problem Strengthens You for Greater Success Ahead

This was one of my self-suggestions for years: *Every problem strengthens me for greater things ahead.* I fed that thought into my mind thousands of times, until it became a deep belief.

For a number of reasons, I would never have made the largest sale I ever made unless I had previously suffered a huge setback.

Remember my sharing the $600,000 payment default that I sustained when a person who owned a chain of car dealerships and was selling my courses to other dealers went broke? Well, fast-forward seven years. Through a friend I was introduced to Lew Elbert, director of education and training for Chevrolet. When we were introduced, he laughed and poked me in my chest, and said: "Ron Willingham . . . DynaGroup!" This was a course that the car dealer sold to other dealers before he went broke and couldn't pay me.

"Yeah . . . how did you know that?" I asked.

"I was a regional manager where a bunch of dealers conducted your course," he replied. "In fact, Lloyd tried to hire me to run your courses."

Wow, I could hardly believe it. If he hadn't known about his dealers using my course years ago, I probably wouldn't have gotten to first base with him. You can only imagine how many training companies tried to get his business.

From that relationship we were able to conduct a pilot for twelve dealers. As I mentioned before, their closing ratios went from one in five to one in four. A huge 25 percent increase. Additionally, their negotiated gross profits increased a whopping 31 percent.

For a number of strange circumstances, without the loss of

$600,000 I'd previously suffered, I probably never would have even gotten to see Lew Elbert. Additionally, without the strength I developed in working out of that heavy loss, I doubt that I would have had the ability to call on or sell the Chevrolet account.

As I previously shared with you, based on these pilot numbers, we got a contract to customize our course, and we certified 1,800 managers in 900 dealerships to conduct the course, with more than 28,000 graduates. Our sales and profits dwarfed the $600,000 I'd lost a few years before that.

Every problem strengthens me for greater things ahead! That belief that I programmed into my *I Am* served me back during those difficult times.

In the forty-eight years since I started conducting training, I've had three separate times when I lost about everything I had. In each case it took three or four difficult years to work through and get back on my feet. Each time, I found that the defeat had prepared me to function on a much higher level than before. I was much more creative than before. New opportunities were presented to me, as overcoming the problems strengthened me to handle larger ones. I tended to view the world differently.

This all proves what Napoleon Hill wrote: "Every adversity carries with it the seeds of an equivalent or greater benefit."

Believe You Should Be Compensated Consistently with the Value You Create for Clients

You can earn the most money by following this two-step priority process. I've mentioned it before, but I want to bring it up again, as it's not just something you intellectually know; rather it's believing it that can strengthen your persistence and success, experientially developing it on many levels within you.

1. Your primary career purpose is to create the most value for the most people.
2. Your secondary career purpose is to expect and thankfully to receive the compensation that's consistent with the value you create.

So logically, since you're paid consistently with the value you create, and you create high value for your customers, you should be paid a lot. Sometimes this two-step priority works quickly, other times it takes a while to see the results. Choosing to practice this two-step priority process unites your *I Know* with your *I Am*, triggering strong, positive emotions in your *I Feel*.

You integrate and harness the synergistic energy of your *Head*, *Heart*, and *Soul*, bringing them into a powerful congruence that strengthens your whole *Being*—the *who* you are. It's the *who* you are that ultimately defines your life.

This nonspecific power works behind the scenes, deep in the limitless energy that comes from the Creator of all things.

How to Benefit the Most from This Chapter

I have included enough activities in this chapter to keep you busy for a while. Although I'll ask you to spend a week on it, I recommend that you come back from time to time, read it again, and select some exercises that speak to your needs. The more you learn, the more you'll learn there is to learn.

To gain the most from this chapter:

1. Read, study, and underline important ideas that speak to your current needs.

2. Pick out one or two of the activities or concepts and work on them.

3. Score yourself on the Persistence Self-Assessment, selecting one or two of the statements to work on.

4. Plot your LifeStages and select one or two of the lowest ones to work on, following my directions.

5. Evaluate your practice.

6. Meet with your study group, following the format you've been doing.

Let me conclude this chapter by sharing an observation that 80 to 85 percent of all salespeople underperform. They do this for many reasons—mainly having to do with limiting inner self-beliefs influencing their emotions.

My purpose and passion is to free thousands of salespeople from these limitations, so they can perform on the higher levels that they have the potential to reach.

11

GROW

EXPANDING YOUR CURRENT INNER BELIEF BOUNDARIES

*A particular train of thought persisted in, be it good or bad,
cannot fail to produce its results on the character and
circumstances. A man cannot directly choose his circumstances,
but he can choose his thoughts, and so indirectly,
yet surely shape his circumstances.*

—JAMES ALLEN

What we're prepared to see, we see; what we aren't prepared to see, we can't see.

A group of research scientists at Stanford University once did an interesting experiment. They took just-born kittens and separated them into two groups. One batch was allowed to see only vertical lines as they grew up. The others saw only horizontal lines.

When they became adult cats, the ones that saw only vertical lines were *incapable* of seeing horizontal lines. Likewise, the group that saw only horizontal lines were *incapable* of seeing vertical lines.

There's a word for this: *scotomas*—blind spots in our mental and emotional visual fields. Anything that contradicts, questions, or opposes our strongly held beliefs often is dealt with as if it doesn't exist and gets buried deeply within our mental, emotional, and spiritual storerooms.

We all have scotomas developed through exposure to parental, peer, and various other groups' thinking. For instance, when we've been conditioned to see only the vertical-line beliefs of a Democrat, we can't see the horizontal-line beliefs of a Republican, and vice versa. The 250 or so religious denominations—each with specific dogmas they hold out as their unique truth—tend to prove this point, don't they? We don't know we have blind spots, or they wouldn't be blind in the first place. Because they are outside our belief or knowledge boundaries, it's as if they don't exist. Any mention of them gets our immediate censure.

Out of all your life experience, you form inner beliefs about who you are, what's possible for you to achieve, and what level of success you deserve to enjoy. You unconsciously live out those beliefs in your decisions, goals, expectations, and behaviors, without questioning their authenticity.

We see opportunities, possibilities, or realities only as they fit into our developed *area-of-the-possible*. I introduced this in Chapter 2, but since a lot of time has passed and you've learned a lot of growth steps since then, let's revisit and expand our understanding of the concept. Study the following model again, and see if you don't discover several new levels of understanding your actions, feelings, and abilities.

Our area-of-the-possible is developed by our beliefs about how well or not so well we performed in the past. The programming and conditioning that we've experienced. Things people said about or to us in our formative years. What we believe our parents, peers, teachers, and coaches convinced us we were capable of achieving or deserved to enjoy. Fundamentally, it's the level of self-value we intel-

AREA-OF-THE-POSSIBLE

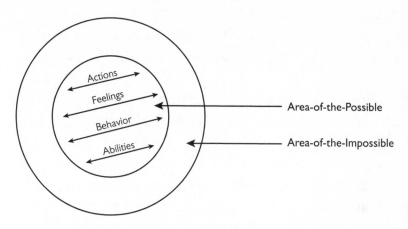

lectually, emotionally, and spiritually bought into from all the messages and experiences that have flooded through our lives.

So in all these life experiences, we form unconscious answers to these questions: *How good am I? How capable am I? What do people think of me? What skills do I have? What can I become?*

We have all unconsciously answered questions like these:

- What level of success do I deserve to reach?
- What level of people am I able to relate to?
- What lifestyle is possible for my family to enjoy?
- What kind of home is possible for my family to own?
- What income am I capable of earning?
- What level of education can we give our children?
- What level of value can I create for my clients?

Whatever your answers are, you accept them as "truth" for you.

You live them out every day in your selling without questioning their authenticity.

But I have good news for you: You're better than you think you are. I like the statement that William James, father of modern psychology and Harvard professor, penned more than 100 years ago:

> The greatest discovery of my generation is that men can change their lives by changing their attitudes of mind.

Actually, the main purpose of my writing this book is to help you expand your area-of-the-possible. Let me stress again that expanding your inner belief boundaries is an *experiential* exercise, not an *intellectual* one. Knowledge alone doesn't change it. Application of the knowledge changes it.

We All Have Our Shibboleths

Shibboleths.

Interesting word. It was mentioned in the Bible in Judges 12:4–6. The men of Gilead used it to test escaping Ephraimites, who couldn't pronounce the word correctly. When they were asked to say the word and said it with an *s* instead of a *sh*, they were caught and punished as impostors.

In time the term came to mean a test word, phrase, or custom that's distinctive to a particular group of people. From locker rooms to ghettos to academia to churches, we form our own shibboleths to define the way we believe things are. The way we see them. The language we manufacture to separate us from other people. The way they fit our comfort zones. The way the world is.

We then treat these beliefs as truth. Sometimes they are, and sometimes they aren't.

But there's even a deeper reason why we can't see what we don't see.

We Have an Inner Need to Hold On to Old Belief Boundaries

Not only do we all have certain belief boundaries, but we often have strong, inner needs to hold on to them. Usually, our belief boundaries don't expand until we release ourselves from the need to hold on to them.

Trey Taylor was enrolled in my course in Atlanta. He and his brother Trent took over their dad's business when their father passed away at a very young age. Trey's father had always encouraged him not to go into that business, so he went to law school and then worked with a consulting firm. Since he was the only one to take over the business, he quit his job and joined his dad's firm, which his grandfather had started. The first few years he had some sales gains, but he felt like they came from the plans his father had put into place. Each year his sales numbers always were just shy of his father's best year.

In the course he discovered a deeply held belief that potentially hindered his success. He realized that his desire to honor his father was causing him to pull back on his efforts to meet and exceed higher goals. A part of him felt he would show disrespect if he exceeded his father's annual sales. It dawned on him that his need was to be a "good son" to his father. He revered his father so much that he couldn't imagine himself exceeding his father's abilities.

He moved past it by realizing that his dad would never want him to limit his own success for the sake of his memory. He then accepted the truth that his father would be thrilled to see him break the old sales records. In Trey's own words, "I consciously put that belief boundary aside and realized that in achieving more, I honor my father more and create my own legacy."

What self-imposed boundaries do you unconsciously build for yourself? What is the real truth about you and your abilities? What might happen if you could expand the boundary of this great wall of your mind? Is there a truth about you that you haven't mentally and emotionally captured yet?

I'm betting that there is.

I'm also betting that you have some deep inner need to hold on to this old belief.

My Premise

Based on observation of many salespeople around the world, I believe the following principles are true about each of us.

1. We each have an inner belief boundary that defines who we are, what's possible for us to sell, and what life rewards we deserve to enjoy.
2. This boundary is based on our past perceptions and not on actual fact.
3. We live out these inner beliefs without questioning their authenticity.
4. We have a strong inner need to hold on to these old beliefs and experience difficulty releasing them.
5. Our sales and life circumstances won't usually change until we release the need to hold on to these old beliefs and move past them.

Just knowing these five principles will do you little good until you take some action that releases you from the need to hold on to old limiting beliefs.

Releasing Your Need to Hold
On to Old Limiting Beliefs

First, understand that your real self-beliefs are well hidden deep within your unconscious *I Am*. Like Trey Taylor, you may need this message to remind you that you have limiting beliefs and that you have some inner reason to hold on to them. Probably no one has ever told you this. I'll share a process with you, and if you truly want to discover and move past some of your past programming, realizing that it takes time and conscious work, that'll gradually help you see progress.

This process begins with your willingness to admit that you may have limiting beliefs and your desire to discover and dislodge or evaporate them:

1. Identify what is or might be an old limiting belief.
2. Say to yourself, "I accept the old limiting belief that [describe the belief]."
3. Say, "I allow myself to have believed it to be true at that time."
4. Say, "I now choose to separate this old perception of the past from my realities of today."
5. Say, "I now choose to let go of any need to hold on to this old limiting belief."

Take a moment and recall what you've learned so far about

self-suggestions. They're statements you choose to say to yourself that describe a positive trait you'd like to possess or develop. When you repeat them over and over to yourself, and visualize the benefits you'll enjoy when they become real beliefs within you, they'll eventually become ingrained as truth in your mind.

Releasing Old Limiting Beliefs is a worksheet that you can download by following the instructions in the Diagnostics section at the back of this book. It will guide you in performing this process. Add your own words to a statement that you memorize. Repeat it several times each day. Inject emotions in your statements. Visualize the rewards you'll enjoy when you release yourself from the need to hold on to old, outdated beliefs—even though you don't now know what they are. With time and this programming that the form gives you, your *I Am* will release it and send it to your *I Know*.

As you perform this process, and as you emotionally accept ownership of the rewards of higher production, or whatever expansion of your area-of-the-possible may bring you, new beliefs will gradually be cemented into your *I Am*. This will then guide your *I Feel* and *I Know* into creative new discoveries. Once your *I Am* is programmed to release the need to hold on to old limiting beliefs, it'll begin to generate the emotional powers to assist you in carrying out that chore. Then, at some point, you'll begin to get hunches or flashes of insight, giving you directions about what actions to take.

Let's think about some other strategies you can use to assist this programming. You can use these strategies by yourself, but they work much better when you're sharing with your study group how each of you is doing them, along with the results you're enjoying.

Your Daily Mental and Emotional Vitamin Pack

Here are six personal growth actions that, when practiced each day, will cause your inner area-of-the-possible to expand. Study them for a moment, and then I'll further explain them.

1. Repeat your purpose statement and accompanying dialogue with the person in the mirror each morning.
2. Review in your mind the benefits you expect to help specific customers enjoy today.
3. Memorize and repeat the definition of client-focused selling.
4. Argue with your negative thoughts or emotions.
5. At the end of the day, list the names of customers you'll contact the next day, what needs they might have, how you might help them, how they might *feel* if you helped them, and how *you* might feel if you helped them. (To do this, go to the Diagnostics section at the end of the book and follow the instructions for downloading the Daily Success Conditioning Forms.)
6. Absorb the beauty of God's abundance.

Write these six actions on an index card or your electronic device so you'll have daily reminders to practice them. Otherwise, days will tend to slip by without giving specific attention to them.

Additionally, your own sense of worthiness is nurtured and fed by this two-step prosperity priority:

1. First, our purpose is to create the most value for the most people.

2. Second, we should expect and accept the compensation or
    rewards that are consistent with the value we create.

This two-step prosperity priority indirectly builds your inner
sense of worthiness. As your inner sense of worthiness increases, it
allows you to discover more of the unconscious blocks, release yourself from the need to hold on to them, and move past them.

Like many other success principles, this can be learned on many
levels, so just because you've read it before, don't dismiss it as knowledge you've already learned.

Repeat Your Dialogue with the Person in the Mirror Each Morning

Remember how in a previous chapter, I shared with you a great
way to get your day started in an energized, confident, anticipatory
manner?

It all begins when you step in front of the mirror each morning,
when the person in the mirror looks at you and says, "Well, good
morning! Who are you and what do you do?"

You smile back and tell him or her your name and repeat your
purpose statement that you wrote out and memorized in Chapter 1
and carry on an index card or your electronic device. Then, have an
ongoing conversation with the person in the mirror. It might go
something like the following, although it will change each day,
depending on current circumstances.

Read and absorb the following dialogue, and then pattern your
own conversation. No, you don't have to memorize and say this ver-
batim; just get the drift, and bring up whatever comes to your mind.

After sharing your purpose statement with the person in the

mirror, he or she will smile and say to you, "I compliment you. You're doing something that's noble and will give you lots of satisfaction and energy." Pausing a moment, he or she continues by asking, "Well, *why* do you do what you do?"

Your response will be: "First of all, my primary purpose is to create the most value for the most people."

"You said 'primary.' Is there more to your purpose?"

"Yes," you respond, "that's my main purpose. My secondary one is to thankfully receive the compensation that's consistent with the value I create."

"That's interesting. Does this mean you aren't all that driven to make as much money as you can?"

"Oh, no, I want to earn a lot of money. I believe I should. But only as a result of the value I create for my customers," you respond.

"Are you kidding me? Don't most salespeople set earning goals first, then sales goals, then activities to reach them?"

"Yeah, I guess they do. I used to do that too. Until I became client-focused and started setting client-focused goals, then sales and activity goals, then income goals, and finally reward goals," you explain.

"Okay, I'm trying to understand you. What happened when you began setting goals in the way you've just described?"

"My income has tripled since I started setting goals like this."

"Wow! You must be pretty excited!"

"Yes, I am."

You'll be amazed at how this morning activity reaches into your emotions, as you look into the eyes of the person in the mirror. In time this nourishes your *I Am*. Your *Soul* knows that what you've just said and thought is congruent with the spirit of truth.

Review in Your Mind the Specific Benefits You Expect to Help Customers Enjoy Today

We all have our morning routine. Getting dressed. Eating breakfast. Leaving for work. Getting to work. Confirming appointments. Driving or going to appointments. Contacting clients for various reasons. Solving problems.

Stop and think about it, and you'll discover that a lot of different thoughts go through your head while you go about your day. Some positive. Some negative. Some just killing time. If you're like most of us, you'll see that a lot of time gets wasted. But here's the exciting, or scary fact: *Our thoughts are the seedlings of our realities.*

Here's another one: *We can choose our thoughts.*

If our dominant thoughts are positive, they'll motivate us to perform consistent positive actions. The same holds true for negative thoughts. All of our thoughts, like seeds we plant in the ground, produce fruit after their own kind. From his classic little book *As a Man Thinketh*, James Allen wrote about the connection of our thoughts and our circumstances. Meditate for a few moments on his words:

> A particular train of thought persisted in, be it good or bad, cannot fail to produce its results on the character and circumstances. A man cannot directly choose his circumstances, but he can choose his thoughts, and so indirectly, yet surely, shape his circumstances.

Few things will give your sense of worthiness daily boosts as visualizing the benefits you give your customers through your products or services. Like the "Joys of Jell-O" lady at the Florida hospital, consciously think of what benefits your products or services give your clients, rather than what they are. Just as food supplements help you enjoy better health in your body, these vitamins help you have better health in your *Head*, *Heart*, and *Soul*.

Also fill your time with thoughts that build your sense of mission. Think of the levels of value you can create for your clients. How they'll feel when you do. How you'll feel when you do. What rewards will automatically come to you.

Here are some general self-suggestions that you can feed your mind:

1. "I enjoy contacting as many people as possible, to see who needs my help."
2. "People welcome me when they know that my goal is to help them if they need my help."
3. "People could suffer serious problems unless I help them."
4. "I should be highly compensated as proof of the high value I create for clients."
5. "Even when people don't need my help, they appreciate my desire to help them—so in a sense I've made a sale that might help me in the future."
6. "I have unlimited income possibilities, because of my unlimited ability to create value for customers."
7. "I become a student of everyone I meet."
8. "When I sincerely care about helping people, they intuitively get the message."
9. "I continually look for people for whom I can create the most value."
10. "I feast my eyes on prosperity and abundance daily."

As you feed these positive thoughts to yourself, over and over, you'll soon find them motivating your actions and expanding your area-of-the-possible. Pick out one or two of them to emphasize. This way you don't get scattered and unfocused.

Memorize and Repeat the Definition of CLIENT-Focused Selling

Client-focused selling is liberating for salespeople. It's internally rewarding. It's transformational. When you do it, your emotions tell you that it's the right thing to do. It releases you from having to "score," which often sets up fear situations. By taking the focus off yourself and putting it on your customers, you sell more. Instead of using fear energy to persuade people to buy from you, you now use service energy to see if you can help them.

Once again, please review the following definitions. I hope by now that you've memorized them.

1. Success in selling is seeing as many people as you can to see who wants or needs your help. If they want or need your help, you help them. If they neither want nor need your help, you haven't failed; you've succeeded in finding out whom you can help.

2. Failure is finding people who want or need your help, but you won't help them. It's also failing to contact people who might need your help because you're afraid you can't relate to them, or they might think you're just trying to earn money off them.

Why do I keep referring to these two definitions? Mainly because we learn these on several different levels.

1. Intellectually understanding them.
2. Questioning the truth of them.
3. Consciously applying them.
4. Feeling the results of your practice on your own emotional makeup and your customers' responses.
5. Transferring them from simple knowledge to values you believe in.
6. Making them a part of who you are and what you do.

Until they become a part of who you are, woven into the fibers of your *Head*, *Heart*, and *Soul*, you should continue to consciously work on practicing them.

Argue with Your Negative Thoughts and Emotions

Our self-talk—the unsolicited thoughts and emotions that bubble up into our conscious *I Know* from our *I Feel* and our *I Am* as we meet different life experiences—can often inject their venom into us at unguarded moments. The yammering of the pessimist within us can occasionally outyell or outlogic the optimist and get our attention with statements like these:

"I've never sold that much before."
"That's impossible."
"I'll never be successful in selling."
"I probably couldn't get in to see that level of executive."
"The economy is bad."
"I could never earn that much."
"I just don't feel like making calls today."
"I'm not sure that I'm cut out for selling."

These self-talk messages can be actual words we say to ourselves or others that trigger wordless emotions that unconsciously motivate us. We consciously repeat them to ourselves when we catch ourselves reliving old rejections, hurts, or verbal wounds that we've put into our memory banks. At unguarded moments, we occasionally withdraw them as punishment for our defeats or lack of discipline. Whenever we begin a new sales call, we tend to evaluate how we did in past contacts, and we can experience the same emotions that are associated with those moments.

It's not easy to fight these old destructive reminders. You need to view them as bullies hanging around the schoolyard, hoping no one will challenge them because they're actually cowards. We weaken them by using the strength that authenticity gives you.

Here's the process:

1. Whenever you notice negative thoughts or feelings surfacing, stop and challenge them. Say, "Hey, wait a minute! Get away from me! Don't try to dump that stuff on me again. I'm on to your old tricks! What you're telling me about myself has no authenticity."
2. Take a deep breath and go on: "Let me tell you about a couple of times when I successfully did . . ."
3. Quickly describe one or two times when you chose to act in a positive, confident, successful manner.
4. Boldly take the action that the old voice tried to block you from doing.

Mentally rehearse the time you confidently faced a fear situation, what positive action you took, and how you grew as a result. Here's a self-suggestion you can repeat in these times:

If I had the courage to do a past activity like [describe a difficult activity you once chose to do], I have the courage to [describe the activity you should do now].

Courage builds on courage. When you take just enough discipline to get started applying a positive action, you'll usually have the energy to finish it out. Continue these actions, and in no time you'll have developed new, succesful habits.

This is a great discussion you can have with yourself several times each day in between other activities.

Daily Success Conditioning

Here's one of the most valuable, transformative self-management tools that I know of. Any salesperson who does it each day will soon notice significant results in client-focused activities, personal confidence, and a more powerful presence. Not to mention increased sales. It's the daily success conditioning process that you'll find in the Diagnostics section of this book.

It only takes about five minutes to do at the end of your day. The rewards can be substantial. In it you'll write down the following information:

1. Who you'll contact the next day.
2. How you might help them.
3. How they might *feel* if you helped them.
4. How you might *feel* if you helped them.

Why is this so valuable? For one thing, with daily application, over a period of time, you'll program habits into your *I Am*, that will cause strong emotions to be released within you. When continued, this interaction triggers positive emotions that empower you. Here's a list of benefits you'll enjoy as you continue doing the process each day:

1. It keeps you focused on your customers.
2. It increases your own sense of professionalism.
3. It builds positive emotions within you.
4. It tends to neutralize common fears of rejection and contact avoidance.
5. It helps carry out your mission statement.
6. It builds your emotional tensile strength.
7. It separates you from other salespeople.
8. It gives you a quiet confidence that speaks of your sincerity.

Once this activity becomes part of your regular routine, you'll look forward to doing it at the end of each day. Your whole countenance will change. You'll wake up each day with a healthy anticipation. You'll carry yourself differently. You'll speak with more authority. You'll attract people, and they'll want to do business with you.

I've seen salespeople increase their sales around 25 percent when they began doing this daily exercise.

I'm often asked in seminars, "How long should I keep writing this down and doing it?" My answer is, "When you don't want to sell any more, or earn any more, or increase your success . . . then quit doing it! Until then, do it every day."

Absorb the Beauty of God's Abundance

Years ago, when I first learned how to program my mind for prosperity and abundance, I wrote this self-suggestion on an index card: *God has created everything in abundance; I only have to reach and claim that which can be mine.*

In his sermon on the mount, Jesus, among other gems of wisdom, said:

See how the lilies of the field grow. They do not labor or spin. Yet I tell you that not even Solomon in all his splendor was dressed like one of these.

Is there no end to the miracles within our sight each day? It's all around us, awaiting our observation. The Arizona wildflowers in March. Vivid spring flowers popping up from the tundra in the Rockies. A hummingbird slamming on its brakes in full flight. Two mated doves, devoted to each other. A wound healing. Coffee brewing. Two octogenarians walking together holding hands. Timeless music. Healthy animals. Sunsets. Sunrises. Thunderstorms. Snow falling. Ocean breezes.

Seek out abundance. Find a way to observe it. Envelop your senses in it. Capture the essence of it. Search for and accept your inner beauty that we all share because of the same Creator. You are a miracle. You have a creative spirit. You can add two plus two and come up with four. Or get creative, coloring outside the lines, and come up with fourteen, or forty-four. This is what great thinkers do. Thomas Edison. Luther Burbank. Louis Pasteur. Frank Lloyd Wright. Andrew Lloyd Webber. And you [insert your name here].

Absorbed beauty, when received with thanksgiving, increases prosperity consciousness within you.

Creating Internal Conflict

Before we're motivated to take action, there must first be some degree of internal conflict. These are gaps between where you are now and where you'd like to be. What you have now and what you'd like to have. Who you are now and who you'd like to be. There are two kinds of conflicts for salespeople:

1. Negative conflicts—a self-focus that's mainly driven by fear of loss, poverty consciousness, or the fear of some unwanted event.
2. Positive conflicts—a client focus that's driven by the desire to create more value for more people, prosperity consciousness, and the desire to be compensated consistently with the value they create.

We have choices as to which conflict we create. Highly successful people know how to benefit from negative conflict, and replace it with positive conflict.

Creating Negative Conflict

Unfortunately, many sales organizations have high salesperson turnover. At some point before salespeople quit an organization, they move toward survival-focused LifeStages in their career or financial lives. This triggers fear, worry, anxiety, and a host of other negative mindsets. Their self-talk tends toward hopelessness. Their mind-set becomes self-defeating—sapping their energy and confidence. Self-reinforcing—making it difficult or impossible to pull out of that state. Self-blaming—leading to beating themselves up.

In everyday life, our *I Know* asks our *I Am* the question: "What are my real beliefs about my future sales, security, and success?" When fear, doubt, and low expectations exist in our *I Am*, our triggered emotions involuntarily answer that question by communicating to our *I Am*, "Not so good." These answers come from the butterflies in our stomach rather than the words from our mouths. The longer we stay in this state of negative conflict, the more difficult it is to move out of it—it is so self-reinforcing.

Our emotions are so convincing that we tend to believe what the flutters in our stomachs tell us. Left unchallenged, these destructive emotional messages can win out over logical thoughts around 85 percent of the time.

This state is associated with self-talk like this:

1. "I've got to get out and sell something, but I don't feel like doing it."
2. "What am I going to do if I don't sell more?"
3. "How long will my company keep me if my sales don't increase?"
4. "Maybe I'm just not cut out for selling."

We can gravitate into this state without even realizing it. Most salespeople don't think much about their thinking patterns, or their resulting emotions. In his great book *Hard Optimism*, Dr. Price Pritchett makes the point that 70 percent of our negative thoughts go undetected. He adds:

> Most of us don't pay much attention to our thinking patterns. Instead of making a deliberate effort to direct this mental traffic in our heads, we leave it to chance . . . As a result, negative thoughts cruise freely through our consciousness. And we

don't even realize how much we're damaging ourselves or others.

Most of us who sell experience different levels of negative patterns from time to time. Early-warning signs of oncoming negative thinking patterns that need attention include the following:

- Feeling drained of energy.
- Doubting your abilities.
- Reverting back to product- or transaction-focused selling without realizing it.
- Allowing subtle fears to grow and replace confidence.

How can we avoid or move past these common traps and transform them from negative to positive ones?

Creating Positive Conflict

First, let's define positive conflict. Positive conflict exists when you have:

1. A high desire to create more value for more people.
2. High anticipation of being compensated consistently with the value you create.

The stronger your desire is to maintain these belief and thinking patterns, the more you'll be motivated to do the following:

1. Discover more people to make contact with and see if you can help.

2. Look forward to earning greater income because you commit to creating greater value for people.

3. Focus on the rewards you deserve to enjoy when you create more value for more people.

4. View your opportunities through the lens of prosperity thinking.

These four actions can energize, uplift, and enable you. They activate your right brain chemistry and physiology, according to Dr. David Hawkins. This thinking releases endorphins and neurotransmitters within you. Doing good things for you. Giving you a second wind. Enhancing your emotional flow. Raising your selling game. Knowing that you deserve to earn more. Thankfully receiving other rewards that will naturally come to you as you create more value for more people.

Positive conflict, which I also call *creative dissatisfaction*, begins with certain attitudes, values, and beliefs. Here are a few:

1. "My purpose is to create the most value for the most people."

2. "I'm constantly searching for ways to help more people."

3. "I'm excited and expect to be compensated consistently with the value I help clients enjoy."

4. "I appreciate the fact that my company is giving me the opportunity to enjoy a successful career."

5. "Instead of worrying about earning more money, I'm constantly thinking about how I can create more value for people, so I'll earn more."

6. "I give thanks daily for the opportunities I have."

Every step and activity in this book, when practiced, helps you mentally, emotionally, and spiritually expand your boundaries. The purpose statement you wrote out in Chapter 1 sets your direction. The CLIENT-Focused Sales System provided the strategy. The attending concepts, values, and beliefs give validity and integrity to your application.

In Summary

Securely housed inside your *I Am* resides your self-developed area-of-the-possible. This inner regulator continually surveys all your past experiences and unconsciously evaluates how well or poorly you performed. Your assumptions—whether true or false—then form your area-of-the-possible. It's an internal picture of what you believe to be possible, or impossible, for you to sell, gain, attain, or become.

This inner belief boundary is so powerful that it will guide most of your actions, feelings, behavior, and abilities to reach only those goals you believe to be within your possibilities. Shattering scotomas, or peeling the walls of separation from your blind spots, can help you look past your limitations and identify strengths you have that can move you into new levels of productivity.

Tragically, most people underevaluate their actual abilities and possibilities. I say this after having more than 1.5 million people go through our courses. Human nature seems to dwell on a handful of mistakes and defeats and ignore boatloads of successes, abilities, and noble acts.

Although not based on truth, our life programming develops mental and emotional boundaries. When we get close to the outer edges of it, we tend to shut down as if the wall is impenetrable. We often give up in the face of this seeming insurmountable barrier.

Until our area-of-the-possible expands, our productivity will stay pretty much the same as it's been.

Remember, developing our abilities only changes *experientially*— by taking action, and applying positive, client-focused activities over a period of time. If you're like me, this chapter gives you enough material to keep you busy for a lifetime. Why? Because I have a saying: "The more I learn, the more I learn there is to learn." Or said another way, "The more I learn, the more I learn that I don't know."

So we become lifetime students.

Our mental paradigms, our areas-of-the-possible, the values, beliefs, and spiritual encoding in our *I Am* dimensions all coalesce into *who* we are. As we're able to integrate our *Head, Heart,* and *Soul* into greater harmony, we automatically expand our boundaries, increasing and deepening our emotional health and quality of life.

This is a nonspecific truth that few people understand, and almost no training and development provides it.

How to Benefit the Most from This Chapter

Review the chapter this week, marking up important passages and making notes to yourself.

1. Reflect on what your area-of-the-possible might be, defining it the best way you can.
2. On an index card or your electronic device, write out the six Daily Mental and Emotional Vitamin Pack actions, selecting one or two each day to focus on.
3. Meet with your study group this week, sharing how you applied the concepts in this chapter and what you learned.

Practicing these actions will help get you started toward scaling the walls that have previously encircled you and shut you in.

My friend and the founder of Kids at Hope, Rick Miller, suggests, "To be able to see the future, a truly human ability, the brain must retrieve information from the past. This is called *episodic* memory— the ability to recall past events and create future scenarios. This is a personal story of who we are, where we've come from and where we're going. In contrast, *semantic* memory is the ability to recall facts and figures. . . . Hope is defined as the ability to visit your future, return to the present, and prepare for the journey—*episodic* memory."

The activity exercises of this book will help you retrieve information from the past, visit your future, return to the present, and prepare for an expanded success journey.

It seems to me that we are all hardwired by our Creator with unlimited potential, but the proper software needs to be developed for this to happen.

12

LIBERATE

ERASING SPIRITUAL AND
EMOTIONAL SCAR TISSUE

*He that cannot forgive others, breaks the bridge over which he
must pass himself; for every man has the need to be forgiven.*

—LORD HERBERT

Whatever damages your sense of worthiness damages your sales abilities.

"It happened when I was five years old," Cynthia Caucci wrote in her letter to me. "My mother and father decided to end their marriage. I was their only child and was used as a pawn by both. I remember sitting in a room with my mother on one side and my father on the other, and being asked, 'Which one of us do you want to live with?'

"What five-year-old can possibly answer a question like that? I did the only thing I could in my young mind, and ran to my mother seeking support. My father saw it as rejection. My mother gave him a 'she loves me more than she loves you' look. My father then left, started a new family, and I never saw him again.

"He died in 2005, and his brother contacted me before he passed. He said my father had suffered a stroke and wouldn't live another 24 hours. My uncle said he had asked for me to come and see him. I didn't go. He passed, and I thought it was all over. In reality, I had folded all the hurt up in a neat little package and tucked it away. Or I thought I did.

"If I had it to do over again, would I do the same thing? Maybe . . . I really didn't feel anything for him, except rejection.

"Now, seven years later, I spoke about this in our last session of your course, and had a breakthrough. I realized that it most certainly affected me, then and throughout my lifetime.

"I visited his grave yesterday, and took fresh flowers to him. I sat there at his grave site and cried and forgave him. I felt a rush of calmness and could hear him say, 'I love you Cynthia.' How I needed to hear those words my whole lifetime."

She concluded her letter by saying, "I've accepted the things I cannot change, and am changing the ones I can."

Here's the great lesson we all need to learn: While we can't change past hurts, we can change our responses to them. That's what this chapter is about—giving you tools to change or neutralize the effects of old hurts or pain. Why do I bring up this subject in a sales book? Because old spiritual and emotional toxins may well influence your sales productivity more than any other factors.

Think about that for a moment. I'll bet you've never heard that before in a sales book.

Hooray for Cynthia for having the courage to dredge up an old hurt and deal with it. She will mark the date she visited her father's grave site as a huge turning point in her life.

You read in an earlier chapter how Cynthia and her husband, Pete, closed a very large sale by practicing the six-step CLIENT-Focused Sales System. But it wasn't just learning the system that gave them that success; rather it was because of the people they became once they improved their sense of self-worth.

Emotional and Spiritual Cancers

Anything that affects our inner sense of worthiness affects our sales. Hurts like this can create emotional and spiritual cancers that eat at the deepest parts of our *Soul*. Most of us hide or try to cover up the resulting emotional scar tissue, but we rarely know how to remove or erase it. As I've said over and over in this book, our inner sense of self-worth—who we think we are and what we internally believe we deserve to enjoy in the way of life rewards—influences our sales productivity over a period of time more than anything else. This is the most significant factor when it comes to sales success.

As salespeople, we have little conscious knowledge of the internal damage taking place within us because of repressed anger, lack of forgiveness, guilt, or even internalizing rejections from customers. Nor do most people understand the impact that these success killers are having on them. Your *Soul*, your *I Am*, doesn't speak in discernible languages like English, Spanish, or French. It speaks in an emotional language, rather than verbal. We feel loved. Accepted. Rejected. Worthy. Unworthy. Optimistic. Pessimistic. Joyous. Depressed. Guilty. Forgiven. Capable. Incapable.

All of these feelings trigger specific behaviors. Rarely do we question their authenticity. We suddenly feel certain self-value sensations, often assuming that they are proof that we are that way. We tend to buy what they tell us. Who we are. How things are. How they should be. What success level we deserve to enjoy.

Harmony of Our *Head, Heart,* and *Soul* Controls Our Sales Production

When we choose with our *I Know* to think or act in ways that are congruent with the implanted values and the spirit of truth in our *I Am*, strong, positive emotions are generated in our *I Feel*. These emotions then help us overcome the normal fears, dreads, and anxiety that salespeople often experience. Truly understand this and your life will never be the same. Once you know how to deal with the cause of your behavior, you become the master, rather than the slave.

This shatters old paradigms of what causes high sales productivity, sending a whole new message about successful selling.

The next-to-last session of the Authentic Salesperson Course is about releasing emotional and spiritual toxins. Some actions are suggested that I'll share with you in a moment. Members are encouraged to apply one or two of them the week before the session, then come back to the session and report on their practice and results.

Course members learn that until they're able to expunge these negative toxins, they won't be able to practice the sales system most effectively.

Here's an example from Vita Morales, who practiced the action *Forgive someone who has offended you*:

> I had been in an abusive relationship with my ex-husband. We'd been separated for almost three years with no communication. So this past week I called him to tell him that I'd forgiven him. The talk went very smoothly; to my surprise, he even

said he was sorry for all the pain and suffering he'd caused. This was huge, because he'd never apologized for anything in his life.

We spoke for a few minutes, and in the end I felt a sense of relief and well-being. I thought it was too easy to be true, when in fact it was. Later the next day I was checking on my 11-year-old son to see if he had packed for a trip. As I walked in his room I noticed a picture of me and his dad posted on his wall. I hadn't noticed it before.

Looking to the picture, I couldn't control my emotions. A sadness came over me and I started crying. I'd never talked to my kids about the contact with their father. I'd always felt guilty for leaving him, because although he was not a good person to me, he was a good father to them. I'd always felt like I'd taken their father away from them, and they hadn't had a father figure in their lives since then.

I talked to my son about all this, and he told me that it was okay, that he was okay. He told me he liked seeing me happy instead of crying and sad all the time.

I needed to hear those words from him, and it helped me release the guilt I've been holding on to this whole time.

This course has really helped me find myself and release toxic emotions I was holding, and at the same time affecting me in both my personal growth and career growth.

Would it surprise you to know that Vita's sales also began to consistently increase? Even more than that, her whole countenance became more happy and positive. The way she dressed and groomed herself changed.

Most of us accumulate these emotional and spiritual toxins as a part of our human responses to problems and other people. Because they are generally painful to handle, we shove them down into our inner vaults, hoping they'll go away. Without our realizing it, they can block our production as efficiently as if we were locked in a cell, with no contact with the outside world.

Because they have no visible walls, doors, or locks, we have little idea of their power over us.

Toxic Invaders of Our Success and Emotional Health

"Life is a series of problems," wrote Scott Peck in the opening of his popular book *The Road Less Traveled*. He goes on:

> What makes life difficult is that the process of confronting and solving problems is a painful one. Problems, depending upon their nature, evoke in us frustration or grief or sadness or loneliness or guilt or regret or anger or fear or anxiety or anguish or despair. . . . This tendency to avoid problems and the emotional suffering inherent in them is the primary basis of all human mental illness. Since most of us have this tendency to a greater or lesser degree, most of us are mentally ill to a greater or lesser degree, lacking complete mental health.

Well, who of us hasn't experienced different degrees of frustration, grief, sadness, loneliness, guilt, regret, anger, fear, anxiety, anguish, or despair? The longer we live, we tend to experience more and more of them. Who hasn't attempted to dodge or shove these unwelcome toxic visitors out the door and into the cellars of our minds? Out of sight, out of mind, we think.

But not so.

As we store them in the deep vaults of our *I Am* and slam the door shut, they can mold or ferment, eventually spewing out their toxicity, poisoning our spiritual resources, and corroding our inner sense of worthiness.

And guess what? Our sales productivity suffers accordingly. And we have little understanding of what's happening.

Here are some common destructive toxic invaders of your sales success and emotional health. Blocking your higher quality of life. Deceiving you as to your true worth and potential. Creating negative conflict in you. Robbing you of the success levels you're capable of achieving.

1. Anger toward self and others.
2. Unresolved guilt.
3. Lack of forgiveness toward self and others.
4. Inattention to basic values of truth, honesty, and integrity.
5. Toxic relationships.
6. Anxiety over possible future problems.
7. Destructive habits.
8. Self-focused "taker" orientation.
9. Blaming other people for our own unhappiness.
10. Allowing ourselves to play the role of victims.

Addressing these issues is never easy, partly because our own egos are involved. Our lowered sense of self-worth has emotionally or spiritually weakened us, allowing these toxic invaders to hang around, like a shiftless cousin who drops in to "only spend a few days" with us. We adjust to them. Unconsciously accommodating them. Hoping they'll leave soon. But they hang around until we help them pack their bags and wave good-bye to them as they drive off.

Our lack of response to these common life challenges builds up, making it more and more difficult to face and address them. Who wants to admit that we were wrong? To apologize? To admit our imperfections? To face our own weaknesses? To show our own vulnerabilities?

Who finds it easy, when another person has offended or damaged us, to go with a humble spirit—not seeking to blame or to defend our own rightful claim against them—but to forgive and clear the air? Is there anything in our human relationships more difficult than this?

Or, on a deeper level, how often do we carry around unresolved guilt? How prone are we to beat ourselves up for mistakes of the past? For many years it was easy for me to accept guilt, because it was congruent with my father's verbal and physical abuse and their messages to me while growing up.

It's only been the spiritual relationship that I have with Jesus Christ that allows me to accept the forgiveness and the unconditional acceptance of the Divine Creator. To focus on God looking at me and seeing the perfection of his Son, and overlooking the trashy stuff in my life as if it never existed, causes me no end of joy and thankfulness. If the Creator of all things gives me forgiveness and unconditional acceptance, why would I harbor guilt? Why wouldn't I hold and demonstrate the most thankful attitude possible?

I must admit that it took a long time to get to this point of spiritual maturity.

How is it easy for us to expect unconditional acceptance from our friends but not be so free to give it back to them? How adept are we at forgiving ourselves? Can we forgive others if we can't forgive ourselves? And vice versa?

Unresolved guilt is an acid that corrodes our physical, emotional, and spiritual batteries. Too often, we suck it up and put on a brave face, which only adds to the pressure of our emotional and spiritual baggage.

Do we allow negative people into the inner walls of our psyche? Most of us have oppositional contrarians—friends or family whose main goal is to see that we don't reach our goals. These are "Yeah, but . . ." people. Whatever you tell them, their response is, "Yeah, but . . ." They finish their sentences by sending verbal or nonverbal torpedoes at your vulnerable emotional underbelly. They then use this as a chance to set you straight, establishing their perfection compared with your weaknesses.

How often do "friends" seem to deal with their own insecurities by pointing out your imperfections? How many of us, who are prone to avoid confrontations, allow them to get by with the subtle depth charges that they attempt to ram down our throats?

How much time and energy do we spend bringing our yesterdays and tomorrows into our todays? This is a great recipe for emotional and spiritual indigestion.

But we don't have to suffer these self-destructive behaviors.

We Each Make Decisions

Many of us make self-destructive choices each day. We may choose to do the following:

1. Hold grudges or not forgive another person.
2. Avoid managing our anxieties in productive ways.
3. Allow other people to invade our space or not respect our personal boundaries.

4. Blame the wrong causes when we don't make sales.
5. Make claims we can't keep.
6. Harbor guilt or self-depreciation.
7. Compare ourselves with others and come off second best.
8. Express anger in harmful ways to ourselves and others.

Our egos being what they are, it's not easy to forget our pride and deal with these issues.

We Create Situations That Support Our Beliefs

The more we play these games with ourselves, the more they create spiritual canker sores in our *I Am*. The more our inner powers are tarnished, the more they erode, and the more we lose the strength and will to deal with the causes. A negative cycle begins. We play the blame game. Our self-value begins limping through our days.

I do it a lot. There was a time in my life that I lost a lot of money and blamed it on a bad economy, and that was partly true. But the deeper reason was that I hadn't handled my finances right. I had made bad decisions, spent too much, and taken on too much debt. When my income quit supporting the debt, I got in trouble and lost millions.

After moving through the denial, anger, and depression stages, I finally accepted responsibility for this financial calamity and began to seek the hidden blessing in it. The emotional agony, self-blame, anger, and anxiety that followed motivated me to want to move past all the hurt and search deeper for the true meaning of it all.

I began to accept that all of this happened for a reason. I do believe in divine providence and that God directs our lives so growth can come. What I've learned in coping and working through all this has prepared me to understand deeper issues that drive our behavior.

It caused me to accept full responsibility for making the most of circumstances—no matter whether they are good or bad. To open my intellectual, emotional, and spiritual ears. To disturb my natural comfort zones. To admit that there's a lot I don't know. To share with others who sincerely want to learn. I now realize that I couldn't have written this book had I not gone through those emotionally wrenching losses and experiences.

How many salespeople do you know who also play the blame game? "I'm working as hard as I can now." "My manager has me doing so many details that I don't have time to call on my customers." "Our pricing is still out of line in this market."

Argue with Your Limiting Self-Assumptions

We've thought about this before, but let's spend a bit more time thinking about the process of arguing with your negative or limiting self-assumptions. Take a moment and review it here. This is a great habit to develop.

Here's the process:

1. Whenever you notice negative thoughts or feelings surfacing, stop and challenge them. Say, "Hey, wait a minute! Get away from me! Don't try to dump that stuff on me again. I'm on to your old tricks! What you're telling me about myself has no authenticity."
2. Take a deep breath, and go on: "Let me tell you about a couple of times when I successfully did . . ."

3. Quickly describe one or two times when you chose to act in a positive, confident, successful manner.

4. Boldly take the action that the old voice tried to block you from doing.

Whenever you discover that you're not reacting to situations with truth and honesty, stop and give yourself a sound reason why your thinking is out of whack.

Seek the truth about yourself. Having the courage to face the truth is not easy at times, but it gets easier each time we do it. As you make yourself do the fourth step, in time you'll notice that difficult things get easier and easier.

Looking Within Yourself

If you believe it's time for total honesty, forfeiture of ego, and a genuine desire to clean out your emotional and spiritual gutters, the following process will have great benefits for you. To the extent you are willing to do this, the effects of your past toxin-producing decisions can be expunged. Removing the lingering hurt of these blockages can open the floodgates of dynamic new levels of physical, emotional, spiritual, and financial abundance.

The fullest measures of success and emotional health will escape you until these channels are cleaned out. Please take some time and honestly respond to the following assessment, filling in the blanks as appropriate.

Making Important Choices

Dr. Viktor Frankl once wrote:

> Between stimulus and responses there is a space. In that space is our power to choose our response. In our response lies our growth and power.

How often do we lash out, avoid, not allow into our emotional space, and punish people for hurts other people caused us to have? As you think about this, take a few moments and recall an angry moment when you either lashed out, spoke harshly to another person, or repeated some juicy gossip.

What if you had taken a moment, a deep breath, and asked yourself, "What is the most positive spin I can put on my urge to attack or react in a negative manner?"

So, when you're tempted to react negatively, take a moment or two and choose your response. What is the most positive spin you can put on your response?

Radical Self-Assessment

Please read each statement and ask yourself, "How descriptive is this statement of my actual sales behaviors?" If it's always descriptive, circle 10; if it is never descriptive, circle 1; if it's sometimes descriptive, circle the appropriate number in between.

1. I am well aware that I must clean out the cancer of toxic emotions before I can enjoy higher levels of sales success.

   1   2   3   4   5   6   7   8   9   10

2. I am willing to move past my own ego and pride, taking responsibility and not blaming other people or circumstances.

1 2 3 4 5 6 7 8 9 10

3. I have offended _____, and I am willing to go to him or her and ask for forgiveness.

1 2 3 4 5 6 7 8 9 10

4. I still hold a grudge against _____, and I am willing to erase this and go to that person, share my hurts with him or her, and let that person know that I have forgiven him or her.

1 2 3 4 5 6 7 8 9 10

5. I am willing to continually discover old wounds that need healing in order for me to reach the sales or personal growth goals I've set.

1 2 3 4 5 6 7 8 9 10

6. I am willing to correct the bad sales activity of _____ _____ and will do it immediately.

1 2 3 4 5 6 7 8 9 10

7. I will correct the bad habit of _____ _____ today.

1 2 3 4 5 6 7 8 9 10

8. I will confront my toxic relationship with _____ _____ and let that

person know that his or her invasion of my boundaries is
no longer allowed.

1   2   3   4   5   6   7   8   9   10

9. I will no longer allow _____
   to dump _____
   on me, and I will seek a spiritual solution to resolve any
   self-inflicted guilt I have.

1   2   3   4   5   6   7   8   9   10

10. I commit to the attitude of _____
    that will help me keep my emotional, relationship, or spir-
    itual channels clear.

1   2   3   4   5   6   7   8   9   10

   Total: _____

Now that you've thought about and made these commitments
to remove toxic emotions, self-beliefs, or relationships from your
life, please review them. Then select two immediate actions to clean
them out.

Now write out your commitments here:

1. I commit to taking the action of _____
   with [name of person] _____, and I will
   do it by this date: _____, 20__.
   When I do this, I will enjoy the following emotional, spiritual,
   or relationship release: _____

   _____.

2. I commit to taking the action of _____
    _____
    _____, and I will do it by this date:
    _____, 20__.
    When I do this, I will enjoy the following emotional, spiritual,
    or relationship release: _____
    _____.

Actions to Practice This Week

Here are some specific actions you can take this week. Taking them
can help you clean out old toxic emotions or relationships.

1. Go to a person from whom you are estranged or whom
    you have offended and, without any defensiveness, admit
    what you've done and ask for their forgiveness.
2. Go to a person who has offended you, and honestly, sin-
    cerely tell them how you were offended and that you have
    forgiven them.
3. Select one habit to break or activity to begin that will help
    others and cause you to feel better about yourself.
4. Confront a person who attempts to control you, dump
    guilt on you, or invade your boundaries, and let them
    know that you want to have a relationship with them, but
    their current behavior [specifically mention it] is unaccept-
    able.
5. When memories of an old past hurt are transferred to, and
    inflame current situations, causing you to unconsciously
    deliver negative responses, stop, take a deep breath, and
    choose a positive response.

These aren't easy actions to take. They require courage and self-discipline, but when you take them you'll enjoy an emotional cleanness that will be worth all the effort it took.

The Most Adequate and Realistic Self-Image of All

One more time: Anything that boosts your inner sense of worthiness boosts your sales. Your sales, over the long haul, will be an extension of your inner sense of worth. To quote from one of my old mentors, Dr. Maxwell Maltz, author of the longtime bestseller *Psycho-Cybernetics*. On the last page of this great book he sums up his entire message:

> The most adequate and realistic self-image of all is to conceive of yourself as "made in the image of God."

Then he ends the book by quoting Dr. Frank G. Slaughter:

> You cannot believe yourself created in the image of God, deeply and sincerely, with full conviction, and not receive a new source and strength.

The actions that I have suggested in this chapter can help you clean out the inner spiritual and emotional sludge and corrosion in your *Soul*, leaving you with more emotional and spiritual freedom.

Personal Growth or Prayer Groups Can Help

Any small gathering that's characterized by honesty, willingness to be open and vulnerable, and unconditional acceptance can be very healthy.

Here's an email I received from Lori Nolan, who was enrolled in my Way to Wealth personal growth course in her company:

> I don't know if I can truly express in an email what this course has meant to me and what this whole experience has been like for me. First of all, I believe in the God that holds everything in his hands, to include my life and everything in it.
>
> At the time of starting this class my life appeared to be falling apart—just separated for the third time from my second husband, you can imagine what a chaotic mess my insides were in. The first couple classes, I was so overtaken with emotion I couldn't even get up and speak.
>
> As my personal world was spinning out of control, I would come to the course on Friday mornings, knowing that the Lord would speak to me about so many things. I looked forward to it, I was comforted by it. I felt good when I was there with my classmates.
>
> Week 7 was really tough for me. I had to speak about a life experience that influenced my self-worth. I told the class about being sexually abused by my grandmother's husband my entire childhood, and how this family secret left me feeling like I was a "black cloud" to everyone in my life for the next forty years. Little did I know then that God was getting me ready to release this awful inner-feeling.
>
> Week 8 was very intense also. Having just experienced eight years of abuse and toxicity with my second husband, it left me

wondering how I could keep making these choices for my life. After discovering what I did about my self-worth, I realized it was because of the "black cloud" theory I had been carrying around all these years. *I'm not worthy of a good, decent man in my life*—that's the thought that went through my mind.

I don't believe I would be where I am today had I left after the first class. It just amazes me . . . I've spent my entire life, so it seems, and thousands of dollars in counseling, and have never gotten what I received from the Way to Wealth in nine weeks.

Thank you again for such a wonderful learning and growing experience. I pray my life will never be the same because of it.

Well, as I'm writing this book, three years after receiving her letter, her whole life has turned around. A happy marriage. A successful business of her own. In writing her to get permission to use her letter, she enthusiastically agreed and said that if her story would inspire others, to use it.

Closing her note, she wrote, "I am as joyful and happy as I appear. I could never dream my life would be this blessed."

Praise God.

Don't Try to Get Rid of Old Negative Habit Patterns; Replace Them with Positive Ones

Want to lose weight? Have you found that the harder you try to lose weight, the more you want to eat? Ever tried to quit smoking? The more forcefully you tried to use discipline and willpower to quit, the more strongly you reinforced the habit and the more difficult it became.

The secret? Don't try to quit doing a negative behavior. The more you try *not* to do something, the more you reinforce the unwanted desire or behavior. Instead, try replacing it with a positive thought or behavior pattern:

- Instead of saying, "I want to lose 25 pounds," say, "I weigh a slim, trim 170 pounds and feel great."
- Instead of thinking, "I'm not a good salesperson," say, "People appreciate my desire to help them if they want help."
- Instead of thinking, "I'm uncomfortable trying to sell to my friends or family, because I don't want them to think I'm just trying to earn money from them," say, "I owe it to my friends and family to help them if I can."

To customize your own positive statements or behaviors, here's a simple way to select them.

1. Identify the negative thought or behavior you want to replace.
2. Define the positive one that you want to replace the negative one.
3. Begin focusing, thinking, suggesting, or practicing the positive replacement.
4. Don't try *not* to do the old negative thought or behavior patterns, but when you catch yourself thinking or doing it, stop and consciously focus on the positive one.

Summing Up

In this chapter, I've presented some deeper causes that influence your sales power. Although they don't seem logical, or even connected with selling, these inner toxins can create spiritual and emotional cancers. Shutting off your positive energy. Choking off your sales productivity. Blemishing your inner sense of worthiness.

Again, anything that attacks or tarnishes your inner sense of worthiness soon influences your sales. Anger, guilt, lack of forgiveness toward self and others, and the other toxins mentioned in this chapter all create inner conflicts. This may be the first time anyone has said this to you. It certainly isn't included in most sales training.

Cleansing your *I Am* of toxic emotions and beliefs can have a huge impact on your life and sales career. Practicing the concepts in this chapter is a way to do it.

How to Benefit the Most from This Chapter

This chapter takes you into some pretty deep waters of self-discovery and growth. The strategies are neither easy nor comfortable, but the inner freedom you'll experience will be worth many times the pride or ego costs. Courage is necessary to perform the suggestions I've suggested for you to practice.

Consider doing the following activities this week:

1. Read the chapter, underlining key thoughts or concepts you want to remember or study more.
2. Score yourself on the Radical Self-Assessment profile, selecting two statements to work on.

3. Select one of the four actions and apply it with appropriate people or situations.

4. Meet with your study group, sharing how you applied one of the concepts or actions of the chapter, and the results you enjoyed. Continue this relationship, conducting it in a noncritical manner, each giving unconditional acceptance to the others.

Many Things Cannot Be Taught, but Must Be Experienced

Now that you've finished reading this book, I recommend that you put it aside for a month or so and then come back to it. But don't just read. Mentally and emotionally absorb it. Learn. Follow the wise words of Anthony Hope, who wrote:

> In the deep, unwritten wisdom of life, there are many things to be learned that cannot be taught. We never know them by hearing them spoken, but grow into them by experience, and recognize them through understanding. Understanding is a great experience in itself, but it does not come through instruction.

In our courses we call it *experiential learning.* Learning by experience, application, and real-life practice. Developing habits, not storing information.

This is why I recommend that you spend a week again on each chapter: rereading, marking, underlining key thoughts. Taking action. Applying the actions in your real-world selling.

I mentioned earlier in this book that I've never reached perfection in practicing the six-step CLIENT-Focused Sales System that I presented to you in Chapters 3–9. After your contacts, check off the steps you completed on the After Contact Self-Coaching Evaluation, which you can download by following the instructions in the Diagnostics section of this book. This gives you a great way to coach yourself and learn from your continual observation.

I continue to learn. I challenge you to do the same. The great John Wooden once remarked, "Success comes from what we learn after we think we've learned it all."

DIAGNOSTICS

Forms for Self-Coaching and Learning

The following process will help you develop strong habits of practicing the CLIENT-Focused Sales System and other skills you learned in this book. Go to authenticsalesperson.com, click on Tools, enter the password *authbook*, and print or download one of the following forms:

1. **After Contact Self-Coaching Evaluation.** Fill out this checklist after your contacts. By evaluating how you did on each of the six steps, you can more easily develop automatic habits of practicing the Action Steps.
2. **Pre-Call and Post-Call Forms.** Filling in these forms before and after contacts will help you significantly increase your natural client-focused skills. Many people in my courses have increased their sales by up to 25 percent by continually using these forms.
3. **Daily Success Conditioning Forms.** Take five minutes at the end of each day and enter the names of contacts you'll see the next day. Continual use of this form will increase your confidence and emotional control and reduce contact avoidance.

4. **Personality Patterns Assessments.** Frequent use of these forms helps you continue to learn about your patterns, as well as those of your clients. You'll connect more effectively with people as you identify their patterns and how they interact with yours.

5. **Releasing Old Limiting Beliefs Worksheets.** These forms help you identify, define, and move past old limitations as discussed in Chapter 11.

AFTERWORD

As I think back over the time I spent writing this book, my hope is that you'll be challenged by the message. That you'll identify and apply the concepts and, as a result, gain new insights into your ability to achieve more career and personal life success.

Has your concept of *success* changed as you've gone through and practiced what's in the book? The spiritual and emotional cleansing that is revealed in our course members' eyes when they begin practicing the CLIENT-Focused Sales System is always amazing. They receive positive responses from clients; they feel better about themselves; they discover increased trust and respect. These benefits—contrasted against our normal ego-focused human nature—stay hidden away from most salespeople.

Allow me to revisit a powerful insight from the beginning of Chapter 2 from Dr. Viktor Frankl:

> Don't aim for success—the more you aim at it and make it a target, the more you are going to miss it. For success, like happiness, cannot be pursued; it must ensue, and it only does so as the unintended side-effect of one's personal dedication to a cause greater than oneself.

Pursue or *ensue*. Incredibly important words for us to contemplate. Both determinants, dividing points, of our lives' directions. Beginning with your client-focused purpose statement, the messages and directions in this book have shared with you the order in which to *pursue* and *ensue*. When your primary *pursue* goals are to create the most value for the most people, success, joy, and self-fulfillment will naturally *ensue*.

It's easy to get this wrong, isn't it? Especially when our definition of success often has to do with new automobiles, homes, positions, or bank accounts. To measure our success by the value we create for others is hardly a popular concept, as it runs counter to our natural self-interested, ego-focused natures. But true happiness and success are *serendipities*—coming to us by indirection as a by-product of the value we create for others.

To *serve* and to be *rewarded*—*pursue* and *ensue*. Which is the *cause* and which is the *effect*? How often do we get these in the right order?

On the wall of a chemical company in Bombay is an old sign that reads: "You must search to find, but not to find what you're searching for."

So be careful what you search for.

If you've benefited from my message in this book, help me take it to more people whose lives would be enhanced by learning and practicing it. My aim is to liberate thousands of salespeople who are in the bondage of transaction-, product-, or survival-focused selling.

If you want to know more about our Authentic Salesperson Course and other courses we offer, and how they can help you elevate your sales productivity and quality of life, please visit authenticsalesperson.com, tenlawsofwealth.com, and money2spare.com.

KEEP LEARNING,
RON WILLINGHAM

THANKS TO SPECIAL PEOPLE

In one of his *Poor Richard's Almanacks*, Benjamin Franklin wrote:

If you would not be forgotten
As soon as you are dead and rotten,
Either write things worth the reading,
Or do things worth the writing.

To write things worth the reading involves others than just the author. So I give special thanks to some people who have footprints all through this book.

First, to all the people who have conducted or been in my courses around the world. Thank you for the feedback, results, and life changes I hear from you. I'm humbled, thrilled, and appreciative.

To Robin Willingham, my daughter, who reminds me how I should have flunked freshman English in college because I don't know where to put commas, what gerunds are, or that prepositions are not words to end sentences with. Thanks for your reading and help, proving that intelligence does tend to increase from generation to generation.

To my friend Trey Taylor for your great suggestion for the

title, and for your dedication to helping people find greater life meaning.

To publisher John Duff for your trust in my abilities to put the book together; and to Jeanette Shaw, for your excellent guidance in editing—your IQ must be off the charts.

Thanks and blessings to all of you.

WANT TO CONDUCT AN
AUTHENTICITY
GROUP STUDY FOR YOUR SALESPEOPLE?

If you enjoyed this book and believe it will help your salespeople increase their sales and professionalism and serve your clients more effectively, then you'll be interested in the *Group Study Leaders' Guide* and related salesperson materials.

Materials Available for You

- **GROUP LEADERS' GUIDE**, outlining interactive development outlines for a twelve-week course
- **SALESPERSONS' PACK**, including book, Success Guide, Pocket Guide, and CD
- **WALL POSTERS**, highlighting the six-step CLIENT-Focused Sales System
- **ONLINE ACCESS TO DIAGNOSTICS**, for self-coaching, activity management, and self-assessments

To learn more about these materials, go to authenticsales person.com, click on Tools, and enter the password *authbook*. You'll find descriptions of the materials and ordering information.